THE CREED IN THE GOSPELS

COLLEGIUM

CHRISTI REGIS

FROM THE COLLECTION OF

GEORGE SCHNER, S.J.
1946 - 2000

THE CREED IN THE GOSPELS

by

ALFONS KEMMER

translated by

Urban Schnaus, O.S.B.

PAULIST PRESS
New York/Mahwah

Originally published as DAS GLAUBENSBEKENNTNIS IN DEN EVANGELIEN copyright © 1985 by Verlag Herder, Freiburg. English translation copyright © 1986 by The Missionary Society of St. Paul the Apostle in the State of New York

Library of Congress Cataloging-in-Publication Data

Kemmer, Alfons, 1911-
    The creed in the Gospels

    Translation of: Das Glaubensbekenntnis in den Evangelien.
    1. Apostles' Creed. 2. Bible. N.T. Gospels—Criticism, interpretation, etc. I. Title.
BT993.2K4513   1986   238'.11   86-12317
ISBN 0-8091-2830-6 (pbk.)

Published by Paulist Press
997 Macarthur Boulevard
Mahwah, N.J. 07430

Printed and bound in the
United States of America

CONTENTS

Introduction 1

Article I	5	Article VII	87
Article II	9	Article VIII	99
Article III	35	Article IX	103
Article IV	54	Article X	120
Article V	63	Article XI	125
Article VI	80	Article XII	131

INTRODUCTION

The title of this book, *The Creed in the Gospels,* requires a short explanation. The book does not claim to treat completely the entire content of faith in a few pages with the help of biblical texts. Its purpose is rather to show that texts can be found in the Gospels which served as sources of the statements of faith that were later put together to make our Creed. These texts will be explained exegetically without trying to trace the lines to the final composition of the individual articles that now make up our Creed. A more complete exposition is beyond the limits of this book; it would be the task of the history of dogma.

In choosing texts the question whether a passage selected was one that gave what are called "original words of Jesus" was not considered decisive. In many cases texts are considered that might be considered secondary on the basis of modern exegetical criteria: that is, they are texts attributed to Jesus by later writers. The Gospel of John has been used as a source though it was composed near the end of the first century and clearly shows later stages of development in Christian teaching. Along with the Synoptic Gospels, the Fourth Gospel is a document of revelation; all four of the Gospels show what the disciples of Jesus believed in the last three decades of the first century.

Since they are inspired writings, they cannot contain error in their fundamental statements. This does not hinder us from reading them with critical eyes; while they have been composed with the assistance of the Holy Spirit, they are still the work of human authors and must be approached as such.

Reference here to biblical texts that later developed into articles of faith does not mean that we are going back to methods of earlier theological textbooks in which the intention was to "prove" individual teachings with the help of texts from the Bible. In these earlier treatments texts were often taken out of their original context and were not understood in their original sense. Such a procedure is not defensible today. As always, teaching of the faith today needs a strong biblical foundation, and this is what the following pages strive to offer. It may be that foundations for certain articles of the Creed appear to be rather slight. Actually, certain positions that have come into question have proved to be untenable. Not all pertinent texts could be treated; texts from the Epistles are rarely cited.

It will be observed that many truths of the Creed are contained somewhat indirectly in biblical statements; their complete meaning was gradually recognized and then later formulated explicitly. Those who share the view of the evangelist John that "it will be for him, the truth-giving Spirit, when he comes, to guide you into all truth" (Jn 16:13) will not consider this acceptance to be misleading.

We need first to explain what we mean by the title "Apostles' Creed" and to sketch briefly its history. The words seem to indicate that this grouping of the most important truths of faith goes back to the first disciples of Jesus. There is even an ancient tradition that the apostles got together before they went out into the world, and each one contributed an article. There are paintings in medieval art showing each apostle with a word-ribbon containing one of the twelve articles. Today we know that the "apostolic symbol," another name for "creed" (in Greek the word symbol means a distinctive mark or a password), developed gradually. It was only toward the end of the fourth century that the Roman Church's form of the Creed came to contain most of the statements of the apostolic symbol.

Its gradual formation corresponds closely to the development of the liturgy of baptism and the statements of instruction for neophytes. There were originally two forms of the symbol: one centered around the mystery of Christ, and the other around the Trinity of God. The Christological forms are the older ones. Though Acts 8:37 is a verse that is missing in the oldest manuscripts and hence indicates a later origin, it does give evidence of the practice in the diaspora around the year 95 A.D. In it the chamberlain from Ethiopia professes his faith before his baptism, using the words: "I believe that Jesus Christ is the Son of God." A further development is given by Paul in 1 Corinthians 15:3–5 as a form of profession of faith handed down to him: "Christ died for us as the Scriptures had foretold and was buried. On the third day he rose again, as the Scriptures foretold, and was seen by Cephas and then by the Twelve."

In 1 Corinthians 8:6 Paul gives a similar Christological profession of faith in God the Father and in Jesus: "We have only one God, the Father. He is the origin of all that is and the one for whom we exist. And there is one Lord, Jesus Christ, through whom all things come to be and through whom we exist."

The Trinitarian form is in Matthew 28:19, in what is called the baptism-command of Jesus: "Go to all nations . . . baptize them in the name of the Father and of the Son and of the Holy Spirit." This verse does not go back to Jesus himself; it was taken by the evangelist from the baptismal liturgy of his community around the end of the first century.

The apostolic symbol was derived by combination of

the Trinitarian form with the Christological one, thus extending significantly the profession of faith in the second person of the divine Trinity.

While it is evident that the Apostles' Creed as we now know it does not go back to the time of the apostles, use of the name "Apostles' Creed" is not altogether incorrect since at least some of its articles go back to the time of the apostles. During the time in which the Roman form of the symbol gained precedence in the western Church, some different creeds came into use independently in the communities in the eastern Church. The Creed used by Bishop Cyril of Jerusalem around the year 350 for instructing his neophytes clearly contains all twelve articles and stands close to the Roman symbol.

The churches of the Reformation have kept the Apostles' Creed, and they continue to use it in their liturgy, with exactly the same words, in some places, as those in use in the Catholic Church.

Besides the apostolic symbol there are others that are considerably longer—for example, the Nicene-Constantinople one that is used at Sunday Masses in many places today. The name comes from the two Church councils of Nicea (325) and Constantinople (381); these meetings of bishops were called to condemn the errors of Arius and Macedonius. As a result, the fathers of the councils added several statements to the earlier symbol.

I

I BELIEVE IN GOD, THE FATHER, THE ALMIGHTY, THE CREATOR OF THE HEAVENS AND THE EARTH

The first article of the Creed was originally a profession of monotheistic faith, in opposition to pagan polytheism. In the ancient Roman version of the symbol we do not find this written as credo in *unum* Deum (I believe in *one* God); it reads simply: I believe in God. Many of the versions in the eastern Church do have the "one God" expression. But the word "one" was later omitted or was considered to be replaced by the phrase "the Father, the Almighty." The paternity expressed here probably refers to the whole world; it does not express the relation of the Father to the Son of God or to the baptized Christians. The word "Father" gains its complete meaning through the second article, which professes faith in Jesus Christ, "his only-begotten Son." The words "Creator of heaven and earth" are also later additions.

In his preaching Jesus often used expressions that we find in the first article of the Creed. The kingdom of God was one of the main topics of his preaching: that kingdom is the eternal sovereignty of one God over the whole world.

FAITH IN ONE GOD

Jesus professed explicitly his belief in the basic teaching of his people: belief in one God. When a lawyer asked him which was the first commandment, he quoted Deuteronomy 6:4f: "Listen, Israel, the Lord our God is the one Lord. You shall love the Lord your God with all your heart, with all your soul, and with all your strength" (Mk 12:28–30). He then adds the command of love of neighbor (Lev 19:18), and concludes: "No other commandment is greater than these two." The lawyer was completely satisfied with Jesus' answer.

The strong emphasis on monotheistic faith probably goes back to the Judaism of the diaspora. The composition of the words of Jesus in Hellenistic-Jewish Christianity came from this source. We can be sure that Jesus shared the belief of his people in the exclusiveness of the supremacy of Yahweh. His words to the man who said to him "Good Master, what must I do to win eternal life?" show this. He answered: "Why do you call me good? No one is good but God alone" (Mk 10:17f).

THE PROFESSION OF GOD AS FATHER

The Synoptic Gospels bear witness that Jesus spoke often of God as Father in heaven. Almost never, though, does he mean by this the paternity of God over the whole world. As an instance Matthew 11:25 can be cited: "I bless you, Father, Lord of heaven and earth." Joining "Father" with "Lord of heaven and earth" can be taken to mean that Jesus wanted to have the name of Father mean the same as Creator. In all other places, however, when he speaks of "my Father" he is stating the special and unique relation that joins him with God. It would be too much to try to cite all the texts that show this; a few can be given as examples.

His prayer in the Garden of Olives says: "My Father, if it is possible let this cup pass me by. Nevertheless, let it be as you, not I, would have it" (Mt 26:39). The parallel text in Mark 14:36 reads: "Abba (Father)! Everything is possible for you. Take this cup from me." The Aramaic form of the word "father" that Mark uses here indicates that Jesus is not addressing God as Lord of heaven and earth; rather, he is speaking to him as his loving Father with whom he has a special confidential relationship.

Jesus taught his disciples to address God as Father in their prayers (Lk 11:2). He also designated God as the Father of his disciples because they had attached themselves to him and thereby won for themselves a closer relationship to his heavenly Father. When he wanted to persuade them to have absolute confidence in God's providence he pointed to the birds in the sky; they neither sow nor reap, and yet "your heavenly Father" feeds them (Mt 6:26). To encourage them to trust in God he brings up the parable of an earthly father who does not give his son a stone when he asks for bread, nor does he give him a serpent when he asks for a fish. He concludes by saying: "If you, then, who are evil, know how to give your children what is good, how much more will your Father in heaven give good things to those who ask him!" (Mt 7:9–11).

When the risen Jesus sends Mary Magdalene to the disciples with the news: "I am ascending to my Father and your Father, to my God and your God" (Jn 20:17), he is not referring to the difference between his relationship to God and to the relationship of the disciples to him; he is simply reminding them of the happy fact that the God of Jesus has now become their God too.

FAITH IN THE ALMIGHTY ONE, THE CREATOR

The juxtaposition of "Father" and "Almighty One" in the first article of the Creed is unusual. Only when God is understood as being Creator of heaven and earth is he also recognized as being almighty.

The word "almighty" (in Greek: pantocrator = Lord of all) is not found at all in the Gospels, and only rarely in the rest of the New Testament. It is used indeed by the authorized version in Luke 22:69: "From now on the Son of Man will sit at the right hand of Almighty God." But the original text says "at the right hand of the Power of God," which is an effort to clarify the common source found in Mark 14:62, "at the right hand of the Power." In this latter phrase "Power" is used to indicate the name of God. There is no doubt that Jesus ascribed omnipotence to his heavenly Father. In answer to the question of his disciples "Who can be saved then?" Jesus said: "For men this is impossible; for God everything is possible" (Mt 19:25f).

That Jesus professed his belief in God the Creator can be seen from the dispute about divorce, where he recalls the original order of creation. "From the beginning of creation God made them male and female. . . . What God has united, man must not divide" (Mk 10:6–9). In the speech about the end of time we read: "For in those days there will be such distress as, until now, has not been equaled since the beginning when God created the world" (Mk 13:19). (This sentence is a quotation from Daniel 12:1 where, however, the reference to creation is missing.) The belief that God created heaven and earth is also given in the commandment against swearing, where we read: "But I say this to you: do not swear at all, either by heaven, since that is God's throne, or by earth, since that is his footstool" (Mt 5:34f).

II
AND IN JESUS CHRIST
HIS ONLY-BEGOTTEN SON,
OUR LORD

Articles 2 through 7 of the Apostles' Creed are concerned with teaching about Christ. This part of the symbol was much enlarged in the course of the fourth and fifth centuries in order to counter the false teachings that endangered the true faith during that time. Articles 3 through 6 deal with events in the earthly life of Jesus. Article 2 tells us something of his nature, while the seventh article is about Jesus' return for the final judgment.

The second article professes that Jesus of Nazareth is the Christ, the Son of God and our Lord. Today when we speak of Jesus Christ, we consider the word "Christ" to be a kind of surname. Originally though it was a kind of title of office. It is the Greek translation of the Hebrew word *maschiach* (Messiah) and so it means that Jesus is the Savior promised by God in the Old Testament. This article of the Creed claims that he was not an ordinary man; he was also truly God. Hence the symbol incorporates statements that are made again and again in the Gospels. The two truths, that Jesus is true God and that he is true man, will be verified with texts from the Gospels, but without the intention to cite all the pertinent ones.

JESUS, TRUE MAN

All the evangelists give strong witness of their conviction that Jesus was truly a man. He was born of a human mother, he was circumcised on the eighth day after his birth, and on that occasion he was given a rather ordinary name, Jesus (Yahweh is salvation). Toward the end of his life he traveled through Galilee and Judea as an itinerant preacher. Finally he was brought before the Roman prefect Pontius Pilate and condemned to death by crucifixion because he was judged to be a rebel and a disturber of the peace. The genuine humanity of Jesus is brought out especially in the oldest Gospel, the one written by Mark. The latest of the Gospels, that of John, points out that Jesus was really human, even though the main stress of John is on his divinity. Three narrations in the Gospels bring out the true humanity of Jesus in distinctive ways: the temptations of Jesus, his agony in the Garden of Olives, and his death on the cross.

The Temptations of Jesus

All three of the Synoptic Gospels have accounts of the temptations of Jesus. The oldest of these reports is Mark's, and it is quite brief. Matthew and Luke give more extensive accounts. In so doing they do not follow Mark; their source was another tradition, and they rework it in different ways.

The Report of Mark
After telling of the baptism of Jesus, Mark says: "Immediately afterward the Spirit drove Jesus out into the wilderness and he remained there for forty days, and was tempted by Satan. He was with the wild beasts, and the angels looked after him" (1:12f). "The Spirit drove" means

that Jesus was impelled by a divine force into the wilderness. He stayed there forty days and was subjected to the attacks of the evil one. In the Old Testament we read of Moses and Elias being in a wilderness for forty days; for them it was a time of special nearness to God. For Jesus, however, the forty days were a period of struggle and of continual temptation.

While it is not explicitly stated that he was victorious in these trials, we can assume obviously that he was. Where the text says that he lived with wild beasts, the reference is not so much to the desolation of the wilderness or the separation from people. The inference is that Jesus' life there was like the life of Adam in paradise. We read in Genesis 2:19f that there Adam lived in peace with the animal world. Because of his closeness to God, Jesus the Messiah also found peace with the animal world.

The prophet Isaiah spoke of (11:6) the messianic time as one in which wolf and lamb, calf and lion, would live together in peace. That the angels served Jesus in the wilderness should probably be taken to mean that they fed him with food of paradise. Jesus is depicted as the new Adam who withstood temptation and won back paradise for mankind. Historical details about the stay of Jesus in the wilderness did not concern Mark. His main point is that in Jesus the new Adam has actually come: he is the one who will reconcile heaven and earth.

Matthew's Account of the Temptation of Jesus
Mark has given us few details of the matter and the manner of the temptation of Jesus; Matthew (4:1–11) pays more attention to such details. The adversary tries three times to trip Jesus, at three different places: in Jerusalem, in the wilderness, and on a high mountain. There is both objective and geographic advance in the sequence. It is also

noteworthy that the entire account in Matthew has a parallel in the fifth book of Moses (Dt 6–8). There we are told about the temptations that beset the people of Israel on their journey through the desert; their trials correspond to those of Jesus. The three quotations from the Bible with which he overcomes the temptations come from the chapters of Deuteronomy that have been cited.

In the first temptation Satan suggests to Jesus that he should change stones into bread in order to satisfy his hunger. In rejecting this suggestion Jesus quotes Deuteronomy 8:3: "Man does not live by bread alone but man lives on everything that comes from the mouth of Yahweh." The topic in the passage from the Old Testament is the hunger that the people of God suffered in the wilderness and the manner in which it was satisfied by manna. Yahweh had led Israel into the wilderness to find out whether the people wanted to live according to divine instructions. God wanted to make them docile by hunger and to show thereby that they were ready to trust in his promises. But the people did not stand the test. They murmured against Moses and Aaron and hence against God.

In feeding them with manna God wanted to show that obedience to him is more important than being fed with ordinary food. The devil, with his tempting words, wanted Jesus to use the miraculous power he had in order to serve his own selfish needs: he wanted Jesus to repeat the manna miracle. By quoting Deuteronomy 8:3 Jesus gives the devil to understand that he has renounced such claims to help himself; he has left it to God to help him in such needs; thus he overcame the first temptation.

The second temptation took place in Jerusalem, at the pinnacle of the temple. Satan challenged Jesus to throw himself down into the temple grounds: God would not permit him to be harmed in such a fall. In this miraculous way he could bring the crowds to acknowledge his messianic dignity. To reinforce his suggestion Satan quoted the Scriptures: "He will put you in his angels' charge in case you hurt your foot against a stone" (Ps 91:11f). It is not necessary to take this scene realistically, as if the devil took Jesus through the air and put him up on the temple roof. It should be taken as a kind of fictional presentation: the devil presented Jesus with an imaginary view of the temple. The temptation consisted in trying to build up Jesus' trust in God to presumptuous trust in God's protection.

Jesus again overcame him with a text from Deuteronomy: "Do not put Yahweh your God to the test as you tested him at Massah" (Dt 6:16). This is a reference to Exodus 17:1–7, where we are told how the Israelites suffered from thirst in the desert and demanded a sign that he was with them and was faithful to his promises: in other words, they wanted God to work a miracle for them. Now, with Jesus the devil is trying to get him to repeat Israel's sin at Massah. Jesus opposes the tempter by recalling the event that is told in Deuteronomy 6:16. Where Israel followed the devil's way and committed sin those ages ago, Jesus now remains true to his Father's wish.

The third temptation takes on worldwide dimensions. This time Satan brings Jesus to a high mountain and shows him all the world's riches in their splendor. The tempter promises Jesus lordship over them all if he will kneel down and adore his satanic majesty. Here too we are dealing with an imaginary scene. No mountain exists that is so high that all the riches of the earth can be seen from it. Jesus again replies with a text from Deuteronomy, where the Hebrew original says: "You must fear Yahweh your God; you must serve him" (Dt 6:13). From its context we see that this command refers to the time when Israel wanted to take possession of the promised land, when there was great danger that they would also be tempted to worship the local gods of Canaan. In fact, on that occasion, the people of the covenant fell miserably and worshiped those gods, seeking to gain their protection. Israel sinned by not having trust in Yahweh and his power.

The situation of Jesus is somewhat like that of Israel. In the second psalm he is told that he should be given lordship over the world: "He has told me, 'You are my son, today I have become your father. Ask and I will give you the nations for your heritage, the ends of the earth for your domain' " (Ps 2:7f). As in olden times Israel sought to make an agreement with the heathen gods of Canaan, so now Satan, the "prince of this world" (Jn 12:31), wanted to make an agreement of the same kind with Jesus. Jesus overcame this last temptation by applying to himself the teaching that Deuteronomy gives for overcoming the temptation to which Israel fell: to serve God alone.

The high mountain that Matthew gives as the place of the third temptation is not mentioned by Luke. The sight of all the riches of the earth is represented as something imaginary, without any kind of bodily transport in Luke's version. In Deuteronomy 34:1–4 we read that God showed Moses the whole country of Canaan from the top of Mount Pisgah and told Moses that all this would be the territory he would give to Israel. Now we have Satan saying that he would give Jesus the whole world.

The story of the temptations that Matthew gives is not an eye-witness account. It was composed in a Christian community in the diaspora for use in catechetical instructions; we should not try to find historical details in it. Certainly it is possible that Jesus experienced a period of temptation at the beginning of his public life. The purpose of the Gospel account is not so much to give explanations about how these temptations were made; rather, it shows how Jesus understood his role as Messiah. He does not want to bring in extraordinary works to prove that he has a mission from God, since he regards demands for such wonder works as coming from the devil.

According to a recent explanation of the temptation story, facts from the later life of Jesus are illustrated in the account of these temptations: we see from other passages in the Gospels that Jesus showed opposition to temptations that were brought on him by people around him. The Gospels give witness that these temptations came even from the closest circle of his disciples. Peter wanted to keep his Master from suffering and suggested that he should venture on a political messiahship. Jesus rejected this unreasonable suggestion with extremely sharp words: "Away from me, you satan (= opponent)" (Mk 8:32f). We find the very same words in Jesus' reaction to the third temptation (Mt 4:10).

Another temptation came to Jesus from his relatives; they wanted him to appear in public in Jerusalem before the Easter festival (Jn 7:2ff). On another occasion his opponents demanded that Jesus should give them a sign from heaven: they wanted him to work a spectacular miracle for them (Mk 8:11f). The early Church may indeed have wondered why he did not reply to this request. The answer to such petitions we find in the account of the temptations as given in our Gospels. By complying with such requests Jesus would have been acting in agreement with Satan and would thereby have shunned the task that God had given him.

That Jesus was tempted to unfaithfulness in carrying out the mandate God had given him by suggestions of those around him is certainly clear from the Gospels. A very early Christian catechist composed the scene of the triple temptation by Satan in order to give an impressive description of the manner in which Jesus overcame such temptations. At the same time the diabolical source of the temptations brought onto Jesus by people around him is clearly indicated.

In any case the fact that Jesus was tempted during his earthly life shows that he was truly human, one "who was tempted in every way that we are, though he is without sin" (Heb 4:15).

The Agony of Jesus

All the evangelists tell us that Jesus was afflicted with great fears of death in the night before he died and that he overcame them in suffering and praying. The Synoptics tell us that this happened in the small estate called Gethsemane (the name means oil-press), where he often went to spend the night while he was staying in Jerusalem. The writer of the Fourth Gospel does not mention the scene in the Garden of Olives; he comes to speak of the similar spiritual struggle of Jesus in a different context. On the occasion of his last public discourse, Jesus says: "Now my soul is troubled. What shall I say: Father, save me from this hour? But it was for this very reason that I have come to this hour. Father, glorify your name!" (Jn 12:27f).

The author of the Letter to the Hebrews also shows that the death agony of the Lord caused his earliest disciples some serious concern when he writes: "During his life on earth, he offered up prayer and entreaty, aloud and in silent tears, to the one who had power to save him out of death, and he submitted so humbly that his prayer was heard" (5:7). Luke's presentation of the scene on the Mount of Olives differs considerably from that of Mark, which indicates that there were different reports of this event very early after it.

Mark's is the oldest Gospel account of the passion of

Jesus, but it is not the report of an eye-witness. Traces of embellishment can be found in it. Probably the prayer of Jesus in the Garden of Gethsemane was a single incident, as Luke reports. But Mark speaks of prayer repeated three times. Even though Mark gives the actual words of Jesus (14:36), we should not infer that he had gotten these words from one of the three disciples who were there with Jesus (in fact, they were asleep—v 37). We must assume that the historical fact, the death anguish of Jesus in this case, was later supplied with somewhat freely-chosen narrative details, as happened also in the story of the temptations.

Jesus took with him three disciples, Peter, James, and John, when he went away from the others before the death agony came on him. The three could see his misery and his extreme weakness; in the passion soon to come they would see even more terrible things. The evangelist uses the words of the psalmist in describing the anguish of Jesus' soul: "My soul is downcast (to death)" (Ps 43:5). He was pushed to the limit of endurance. He left the three disciples and went some distance away to carry out his battle with deathly fear alone. He fell to the ground in a gesture of humility before God. His prayer that the chalice might be taken from him was not a petition that the anguish about death should end; he was more concerned with the trial he would have to undergo before dying.

The symbol of the chalice comes from the Old Testament where the wish is often expressed that God should give the enemies of Israel the cup of his anger to drink. From this we can gather that Jesus was not simply praying to be saved from death. He was also concerned about the judgment of God. If the total humanity of Jesus is expressed anywhere in the Gospel, it is here, for Jesus adds at once: "Not what I wish, but what you wish (should happen)." Even in this final hour he considered his place as the obedient servant of God to whose wishes he was always subject.

The three disciples, whom he found sleeping when he returned from his prayer, offer a complete contrast to Jesus. He gives a reproof to Peter, who only a short while before had maintained that he was ready to follow his Master into death (Mk 14:31); he says: "Could you not stay awake even for an hour?" And to all three he says: "You should be awake and be praying not to be put to the test." This they should do not just out of sympathy for Jesus; they were themselves in danger. "The spirit is willing, but the flesh is weak." It is a warning that has no time limit. Among all peoples in all eras the contrast between good will and earthly wickedness and weakness can be found. We must all pray for the strength to overcome such weakness.

There is a double repetition in Mark's version of the scene in the garden. On his second return to the disciples from an interval of prayer, Jesus says to them: "You can sleep now and take your rest." This may be taken as a bitter outcry, or as a kind of reproachful question. He was now peaceful and prepared, though he knew that the hour for being handed over to his enemies had come. His prayer to his Father had strengthened him.

The parallel account in Luke 22:39–46 is a shortened and simplified version of Mark's. Luke softens the impression one gets of the weakness of Jesus and strengthens the idea of his obedience to the will of his Father. There is question of the authenticity of verses 43f, which tell of the coming of angels from heaven to encourage Jesus. These lines are missing in many manuscripts, and it is quite possible that many of those who transcribed the sentences considered it improper that Jesus would need the help of angels (even though in the end it is his Father who helps Jesus). Likewise considered improper by many is verse 44, which says that after Jesus had prayed more urgently "his sweat was like blood that dropped on the earth." However, this verse only shows that the help of angels did rid him of the agony of death and that it was by his prayer he had to endure these trials. Hence it is more acceptable to consider both verses as authentic than to reject them as statements that were originally missing in the text. To say that the drops of perspiration of Jesus fell like blood to the ground is a rather exaggerated description of his intensive prayer. The admonition to the disciples, "Get up and pray not to be put to the test," is a clear reference to the Lord's Prayer, which, in Luke's version, ends with: "And lead us not into temptation" (11:4).

The Death of Jesus on the Cross

The true humanity of Jesus is shown by his death. In Mark's version this is strongly stressed (15:23–41), and the other evangelists add explanation on many points; John's Gospel particularly brings out the exaltation and glorification of Jesus in his death.

The Gospels do not describe in detail how the crucifixion was done. It was not necessary for them to do so; readers of their time often had opportunities to witness such events. Outside every city there was a place set aside for the execution of criminals. The place of execution outside the gates of Jerusalem was called Golgotha, which means "skull," apparently chosen because of the skull-shaped form of the hill there. Posts were driven in the ground to serve as vertical supports for the crosses. The horizontal cross-arm had to be carried there by the man who had been convicted, which meant an additional great hardship for the man already weakened by scourging. Mark tells us that the soldiers who had been ordered to carry out the execution of Jesus forced a passer-by to help Jesus carry his own cross.

The wine mixed with myrrh that the soldiers offered Jesus was given him to dull his senses so that he would not feel so much the terrible pains of the nails driven through his hands and feet. Mark glosses over the horrible happening with the concise expression: "Then they crucified him." To this he adds what is certainly an historical detail, the sharing out of the clothing of the crucified one by the soldiers, who, by local custom, had a right to them. In this Mark sees fulfilled the words of Psalm 22:18: "They shared out his clothing, casting lots to decide what each should get." He does not quote the passage exactly, but it agrees faithfully with the psalm. What happened to Jesus is seen to be in accord with the divine decree in revelation, and this makes the event easier to understand.

The basis of the judgment of execution against Jesus is indicated by the inscription "The King of the Jews" that was attached to the cross. He was the cause of a political uprising, a rebellion against Rome. The Christians who handed down these accounts saw in this title a deeper sense: as the Messiah he is actually a king. In his account of the passion John has brought out this thought emphatically. Pilate explicitly asks whether he is the King of the Jews, and Jesus answers, after clarifying the expression, with a distinct "Yes" (Jn 8:33–37).

The mockery and abuse that the condemned One is subjected to follows from what was said earlier in the hearing before the Sanhedrin. A false witness said that he had heard Jesus say: "I am going to destroy this temple made by human hands, and in three days build another, not made by human hands" (Mk 14:58). Seeing the helpless weakness of the crucified One, they taunted him with biting ridicule: "Save yourself! Come down from the cross!"

The most abject point in the suffering of Jesus is in the loud cry that only Mark gives us in his "word from the cross." The evangelist gives first the Aramaic expression and translates it into Greek, showing thereby that this tradition goes back to the Aramaic-speaking original community in Jerusalem. Jesus certainly spoke these opening words of Psalm 22, but most likely quoted them in the original Hebrew since the call to God in Hebrew is *Eli* (my God) rather than the Aramaic *Eloi*. If those around him understood him to be calling to Elijah the prophet, this can be understood better if he said *Eli* rather than *Eloi*. We can assume that on the cross Jesus prayed the whole psalm, not just the opening words. Probably the early Church handed down the words of the psalm in their Aramaic form in order to indicate that Jesus not only prayed the psalm but also underwent the experience that the psalm expresses. It must be granted that we cannot say what went on in the soul of Jesus at that time. Many commentators say that his cry was one of doubt and despair; they say that he was actually deserted by his Father in that hour. Others say that he also prayed the second part of the psalm, in which the suffering one expresses his trust in God. Certainly Mark wanted to tell of the deep spiritual distress of the crucified One.

The mistaking of the word "Eli" for Elijah brought one of those standing by the event to dip a sponge in vinegar and put it on a stick to bring it to the mouth of Jesus for him to drink. Elijah, the great prophet of the Old Testament, was considered by Jews of that time to be a helper in every need. Hence people thought that Jesus called out his name begging for his help. Soldiers considered diluted vinegar to be a good drink to quench thirst and give refreshment. The soldier meant well: he wanted to help Jesus, even though he spoke mockingly when he said: "Wait and see if Elijah will come and take him down."

The ancient Church, however, saw in the soldier's act the fulfillment of another saying in the psalms: "They gave me poison to eat; when I was thirsty they gave me vinegar to drink" (Ps 69:22). In their view the giving of the vinegar drink was another torment for the dying Jesus.

"Then Jesus gave a loud cry and breathed his last." The quick and sudden death of Jesus is recorded in this short sentence. While others who were executed by crucifixion had to suffer lengthy torment until they finally suffocated, Jesus died quite suddenly with a loud cry. Probably there was a second cry, as Matthew 27:50 explicitly says. There is nothing to compel us to consider this as an expression of doubt; it could just as well be a cry of victory. This would not lessen the deep distress of Jesus on the cross, but it could signify his justification by his Father in the instant of his death. Luke (23:46) tells us that Jesus died with the peaceful words from Psalm 31:5 on his lips: "Father, into your hands I commit my spirit." John says that he died after pronouncing the triumphal words: "It is accomplished" (19:30).

Even though the oldest evangelist stresses the humanity of Jesus in his account of the passion, he does not omit mention of his divinity. This is shown by what he says directly after Jesus' death. The Roman centurion who saw Jesus die from close-by said: "In truth this man was the Son of God." The manner in which Jesus had undergone the crucifixion had awakened in this heathen the conviction that this Jesus was not an ordinary man: he was someone extraordinary, a godly person (the word of the centurion cannot be taken to mean more than this). It is certain, though, that the early Christian community understood the words of the heathen soldier to be a confession of the divine Sonship of Christ in the proper sense. Even in the death of Jesus there is disclosure of the mystery of the person of Jesus, the mystery that is stressed again and again throughout Mark's Gospel.

JESUS, TRUE SON OF GOD

The second article of the apostolic symbol professes Jesus as the "only-begotten Son of God" and "our Lord," while also describing him as a real and true man. God is not a single person; he is the Father of a Son who is one begotten of him and who is a different person in uniqueness of being. The symbol calls this Son of God "first-born," which is not an altogether accurate translation of the Greek word *monogenes*. *Monogenes* means only-begotten, uniquely born. The term "first-born" is naturally associated with the idea of becoming man, of incarnation, by which the Son of God was born into the human race. This fact, though, is the topic with which the following article of the Creed is concerned. Here in the second article the word "only-begotten" has been added, perhaps to correct certain false teachers of the second century who taught that several divine beings proceeded from the original divine person. In opposition to this erroneous teaching, the addition was made.

The term *monogenes* is not often used in the New Testament. Luke always uses it in the sense of "unique, without siblings" (e.g., 7:12). We find the term used to describe the relation of Jesus to God only in the Gospel of John. Those who believe in God are also described as sons of God, though only by adoption; John always calls them "children of God." For John Jesus is the Son of God (cf. Jn 1:12–14). The description of Jesus as the only-begotten Son has surely been taken into the Creed from John's Gospel.

In calling Jesus "Our Lord" in the second article of the

Creed, the purpose is to strengthen the idea of the divinity of Jesus. The word "Lord" (*Kyrios*) is the Greek translation of the Old Testament paraphrase of the divine name "Yahweh." As the true and only Son of God, he is, like his Father, our Lord.

How the evangelists expressed their faith in the Son of God will now be shown from some texts of the Gospels.

THE PROLOGUE OF JOHN'S GOSPEL

The Gospel that was composed last (around the end of the first century) begins with a preamble (Jn 1:1–18) that does not have a parallel in the three Synoptics. The prevailing modern opinion of scholars is that the author had in mind a hymn then in use in the Church when he wrote the prologue. Passages in the Epistles in the New Testament give examples of such ancient Christian songs (e.g., Phil 2:6–11; Col 1:13–30; 1 Tim 3:16). The verses 6–8, 12f, etc., show that the evangelist supplied additions to the old hymn; they are clearly in prose style and show traces of John's peculiar expressions not otherwise found in genuine verses of the hymn.

As it stands, the prologue does not mention the word "Jesus" or "Christ." It uses the term "the Word"—in Greek, *ho logos*. John does not explain the expression; apparently the community for whom he wrote understood whom and what he meant. What could be the origin of the expression "the Word" has puzzled readers considerably, and there is today no common agreement. The Greek word "logos" does not mean simply "word": it also means "thought," "reason." Already in pre-Christian writings there is mention of "logos." Philo of Alexandria, a Jew who was a contemporary of Jesus but lived in the diaspora and did not know him, uses the word over twelve hundred times in his writings, with several different meanings. In particular he sees in Logos an intermediate being between God and the world, a being who is empowered in the creation, preservation, and government of the world. This being is also charged with the task of bringing mankind into union with God.

That this philosophical Logos has much in common with the one we find in John's Gospel is immediately evident—so much so that certain exegetes say that the evangelist took the term from Philo and applied it to Jesus.

However, the Logos of John's prologue stands closer to what we find in the Old Testament. There we often see mention of the "Word of God," with the meaning that this Word is the governing power of Yahweh in nature and history. It also applies to God's care for mankind, to whom the will of God is manifested by the Logos. John's Logos is even closer to the wisdom of the later books of the Old Testament, where wisdom is described as the companion of God in the creation of the world and is shown as an independent being. Paul applies the concept of "wisdom" to Christ when he calls him the "power and wisdom of God" (1 Cor 1:24).

It is highly probable that the title of Logos in the prologue of John's Gospel denotes Christ as the divine wisdom already acclaimed in the Old Testament. The evangelist calls it Logos rather than wisdom because he wants to recall the statements about the word of God as they are found in the Bible. It may have been that the masculine noun "logos" seemed to him a better word to use than the feminine word "wisdom."

In any case there is no record that Jesus used the word "logos" himself. It appears only twice in the prologue, and never in the Gospel that follows or as coming from the mouth of Jesus.

In its present form the prologue has three clear divisions. The first division speaks of the original being of the Logos (1–4); the second division tells of his coming into the world of humanity (5–13), and the third division recounts his incarnation and its salvific meaning for believers (14–18).

The prologue begins with the sentence: "In the beginning was the Logos." Similarly the first sentence in Genesis is: "In the beginning God created heaven and earth." Genesis says what *happened* in the beginning; John says what *was* in the beginning. He does not want to speak of the origin of the world; he wants to announce the world-to-come of the Logos. The Logos does not belong to the world; he lives for all time and is therefore beyond this world. Hence he has pre-eminence over all creation. The prologue professes the pre-existence of the Logos and his eternal being before the origin of the world.

Furthermore we read: "And the Logos was with God," that is, he was God, in contrast to an independent being still not separated from God. He was not just something divine: he was as much God as the One with whom he existed from all eternity. In this way the prologue tells of the eternity, the independence, and the divinity of the Logos.

The following verses speak of the relation of the Logos to the world and to mankind. Everything that exists, all the works of creation, the whole world has come to be through him. The life of all creatures is contained in him; he possesses all life-giving power. For mankind this life of the Logos was also light. He shares his fullness of life with mankind and gives to persons the light of revelation.

The second strophe of the hymn speaks of the coming of the Logos into the world of humanity. As bringer of light and life, one would expect that the Logos would be received with joy. That this was not the case is indicated in verse 5 in somewhat veiled words: "The light shines in the darkness, a light that darkness could not overpower." By "darkness" here the author does not mean some kind of power independent of the light; he means the ethical-religious situation of mankind that has gone away from its Creator. The world cuts itself off from the light; it does not want to know anything about revelation. The afflictions of the Church seem to be audible in this sentence as it laments the incomprehensible attitude of the world in opposition to divine revelation.

After some intermediary remarks by the evangelist (vv 6–8), in verse 9 the hymn develops further what was said in verse 5. "The true light that enlightens all men came into the world." The old hymn seems still to have in mind the coming of the Logos to all of creation. The evangelist nevertheless understands the sentence as referring to the incarnation, even though this topic is not explicitly taken up until verse 14. The Logos is the name of the true light, the real light which is actually that which can be called light. It enlightens every person, not only those who are believers; it enlightens those who cut themselves off from it. It does not indeed bring enlightenment to them; it only leads them to blindness (cf. Jn 9:39–41).

The world, of which verse 10 says that it does not know the light, is no longer the entire creation; it now means only mankind. "World" here has the same negative sense as "darkness" (v 5). Here also "knowing" does not mean rational understanding; it means willing acceptance of the revelation coming from God. Verse 11 repeats in other words what has just been said: "He came into his own domain and his people did not accept him." Here we take "his own" to be the world of mankind, where his own (literally "the proper ones") are the people. It is possible, however, that the evangelist was thinking of the people of Israel who are often spoken of in the Old Testament as the proper people of Yahweh.

Still it was not the whole world that refused to accept the Logos when he came. There were some people who did accept him, who received him with faith. To those who open themselves to him in faith he imparts the gift of becoming children of God. This means sharing in a new life, being given a place in a new existence. We cannot earn this new place by our own efforts; it stands in contrast to our earthly begetting. It is begetting of God. The believer receives this new life in baptism; the person becomes one who is described (Jn 3:5) as newly born through water and the spirit.

"And the Logos was made flesh." In order to appreciate how ineffable this statement is one must keep in mind what has already been said about the Logos, about his eternity, his divinity, his efficacy as Creator of the world. Now we are told: he *was made* flesh. The tense of the verb that the original text uses here indicates a new, one-time happening, an actual event. The Logos was already present and active in the world. Since he had already run into rejection by mankind, he wanted finally to come in a new, inexplicable way: he would become man himself!

John says plainly: he became flesh. This simply means that he became man; in the Old Testament "flesh" often means a living, animated person, with the necessary side-effects of weakness and frailty. Thus we read in the prophet Isaiah: "All flesh is grass and its beauty like the wild flower's. The grass withers, the flower fades, but the word of God remains forever" (Is 40:6f). In choosing these words the vexations of becoming man are emphasized: the Logos who lived in the grandeur of God now takes on the lowliness of human existence.

"And he has lived among us." As once Yahweh lived among the wandering folk of Israel in the "tent of revelation" in the desert, as the nomad people of Palestine live close together in tent communities, so by his incarnation the Logos has walked among us in closest community. "And we saw his glory": so do all those who have received him in faith profess him in grateful joy in their communities. With the eyes of faith not only those who were eyewitnesses of the earthly Jesus profess his glory; all the later Christians also do so.

In the Old Testament "glory" meant the external manifestation of the majesty of Yahweh as he came close to them in fire and in clouds. In John's Gospel Jesus manifests his glory especially in signs—that is, in the miracles he worked (cf. Jn 2:11). This glory was not, indeed, perceptible by bodily eyes; the "flesh" he had taken up hid it. Only after his return to the Father did Jesus look for this glory for his humanity too (cf. Jn 17:5). Here, therefore, the sight is not meant to be for the eyes of the body; the reference here is to a perception of invisible reality.

This glory belongs to the incarnate One as the "only Son of the Father," who is grace and truth. In the Old Testament already we find this related pair of concepts "grace and truth" used to describe the nature of God as it is effective in mankind. The Logos is full of grace because he is life; he is full of truth because he is the light. With the word "only-begotten" that the original text uses here, the unity of the historical Jesus with the Logos existing eternally with God is stressed.

"No one has ever seen God; it is the only-begotten Son, who is nearest the Father's heart, who has made him known." This last verse of the prologue once again takes up the concept of the "only-begotten" One, and adds "who is God" (translations differ somewhat at this point). In any case, in this concluding verse John is saying: no earthly person can see God and discern what he really is, so he cannot tell what his nature is. There is now one reliable revealer of God: his co-natural Son "who is nearest to the Father's heart," who lives in closest community with him for eternity, and who, as one who became man, is now, after his ascension, also with him in a natural human state. He is the only absolutely reliable messenger of God. The divine dignity of the One who became man cannot be expressed more strongly and plainly.

The Baptism of Jesus

All three of the Synoptic Gospels tell us that at the beginning of his public life Jesus was baptized in the Jordan by John the Baptist. That the early Church invented this story is unthinkable. The baptism by John brings up a serious question: Why would Jesus want to undergo the baptism of penance? Did he want to acknowledge that he was a sinner?

The meaning of the baptism of John cannot be determined with certainty. According to Mark 1:4 the Baptist preached "a baptism of penitence for the remission of sins." Did the baptism or the penitence effect the remission of sins? Most likely the penitence was the effective part. A person proclaims penitence and readiness for conversion by coming forward and asking for baptism. Forgiveness of sins is merited by this public willingness to be baptized. On the basis of conversion to God he gains the forgiveness of sin; the baptism gives him assurance that his conversion has been recognized by God. The ablution in the waters of the Jordan was also a seal of the forgiveness that the one baptized received in conversion. Obviously the evangelist Matthew does not consider the baptism of John to be a sacrament that takes away sin, for in the parallel passage (3:1) the words "for the forgiveness of sin" are omitted. He does attribute the power to forgive sins to the blood shed by Jesus (26:28).

In a dialogue that only Matthew gives (3:14f) at this point in the narrative, he indicates that he considered the baptism of Jesus by John to be a problem. He wants to explain in this exchange between Jesus and John how Jesus can receive the baptism of penitence without losing his preeminence over John. Even before Jesus came to him, John said to his hearers: "I baptize you in water for repentance, but the one who follows me is more powerful than I am. . . . He will baptize you with the Holy Spirit and with fire (Mt 3:11). Hence he hesitated to baptize Jesus, and protested: "It is I who need baptism from you, and yet you come to me!" Jesus' reply is: "Leave it like this for the time being; it is fitting that we should, in this way, do all that righteousness demands" (3:14f). The meaning is: complete righteousness consists in doing what God asks of us. It is his will that Jesus should put himself as one in the line of sinners and allow himself to be baptized by a lesser one. It would seem that Matthew added this interchange in order to stress the greater dignity of Jesus even while Jesus took what seemed a lower place among the humbler ones.

Directly after the baptism the evangelist tells of a revelation of God that attests to the baptismal event. Three acts are included in this sign of divine approval: the opening of heaven, the descent of the Holy Spirit, and the proclamation by a heavenly voice.

"He saw the heavens opened" (Mk 1:10). In the original text the passage speaks of the heavens opening themselves, which could be a reference to Isaiah 63:19: "Oh, that you would tear open the heavens and come down!" The yearning call of the prophet of Advent for the coming of the Messiah is now fulfilled in the baptism of Jesus. The opening of the heavens announces that God has now begun the time of salvation.

"And the spirit, like a dove, descended on him." This sentence also recalls places in the Old Testament where the Spirit of the Lord is mentioned, the Spirit who comes to help the Messiah in his task (cf. Is 11:2). The symbol of the dove, whose descent on Jesus declares the coming of the Spirit, recalls Genesis 1:2, where we read that the spirit of Yahweh hovered over the waters (like a bird). It should be noticed that the passage reads: "the Spirit came *like* a dove"; it does not say that the Spirit took the form of a dove. In order to represent the coming of the Spirit in some way the symbol of the dove was a handy one to use to allegorize for the Jews the presence of God.

"And a voice came from heaven, 'You are my Son, the Beloved; my favor rests on you.' " This is a clear reference to Isaiah 42:1: "Here is my servant whom I uphold, my chosen one in whom my soul delights. I have endorsed him with my spirit." Where Mark uses the second person (*You are* . . .), this is a reference to Psalm 2:7: "He has told me, 'You are my son . . .' " The divine voice from heaven wishes to show that Jesus is not only a servant of Yahweh; he is also the beloved and only-begotten Son.

How should we explain this theophany, this appearance of God? Many interpreters say that it was given for the benefit of the people present, so that from the very beginning Jesus should be recognized as the Son and the Messiah sent by God. But neither Mark nor Matthew mentions the presence of other people at the baptism of Jesus. Luke indeed writes that "while all the people were being baptized Jesus was baptized too" (3:21), but he does not say that the crowd of people saw or heard anything remarkable. According to John 1:32 only the Baptist saw the Spirit come down from heaven like a dove and rest on Jesus. John does not have anything to say about the opening of the heavens or the voice of God. We can infer from this that the theophany applied to Jesus alone.

But then we are inclined to ask: What could it mean for him? One explanation says that it was only from this experience after his baptism that Jesus became aware that he was the Son of God, the Messiah. Another interpretation sees in this scene the adoption of Jesus as the Son of God. Both these explanations must be rejected. Surely Jesus knew before that he had been given the messianic task to do; all the evangelists see him as the true and real Son of God, not an adopted one. At most one can say that in the voice from heaven Jesus received the commission to begin his messianic work.

A newer interpretation is gaining preference; it considers the story of the theophany to be an early Christian expression of belief, not an exposition of an historical event. It was intended for the first readers and hearers of the good news, so that from the very beginning they should know who and what Jesus actually was. They needed some impressive evidence that he was the beloved Son of God. Hence we find in Luke and in Mark the stress on the familiar "thou": "Thou art my beloved Son." In this way Jesus is raised not only above the other people being baptized; his pre-eminence over the Baptist is also emphasized.

Thus one can say: the story of the theophany on the occasion of the baptism of Jesus plays the role of a written evidence that presents to us the unique dignity of Jesus. This explains also the many references to Old Testament texts. The humbling of himself that Jesus underwent when he allowed himself to be baptized by John did not keep the faithful from professing him to be the beloved Son of God.

Mark gives us another account of a theophany in a later chapter (9:2–10) on the occasion of the transfiguration of Jesus. There on the mountain the glory of God also appeared, this time in the form of a cloud, from which a voice cried out: "This is my Son, the Beloved. Listen to him." Again, this account cannot be one given by an eyewitness. It is a creation of the early community: an expression of their faith in the divine sonship of Jesus. As Jesus himself used parables in his teaching to bring to his people higher truths through such stories, so here the author of these accounts felt justified in using this method to express the faith of the Church in the divinity of Jesus.

III
CONCEIVED
BY THE HOLY SPIRIT
BORN OF THE VIRGIN MARY

The third article of the symbol is concerned with the earthly coming of Jesus: his conception and birth. It tells us that he is not the son of Joseph; he was conceived through divine omnipotence in a miraculous way in the womb of Mary, so that she is his virgin mother. Here the Creed simply follows the account of Luke's Gospel, in which the first chapter tells of the annunciation to Mary and of the birth of Jesus. Matthew's account must also be considered, since there also we are told of the origin of Jesus, but from another source.

THE CONCEPTION OF JESUS

The childhood Gospel of Luke (Chapters 1 and 2) differs significantly from the later chapters. Modern exegesis is almost unanimous in saying that the evangelist found these chapters already written in Greek and put them at the beginning of his Gospel with only slight changes in their text. The manner of reporting in these chapters shows strong resemblance with the language of the Greek translation of the Old Testament, which is called the Septuagint. Probably the author was a Jewish Christian in the diaspora who followed closely the language of this translation of the

Bible. Possibly, however, the two chapters could have first been composed in Aramaic or in Hebrew.

The construction of the two chapters is quite ingenious. The events of the life of John the Baptist are placed in parallel with those of Jesus' childhood, in which it is shown that what happened to Jesus always excelled by far the corresponding event in the life of John. The successive events of the annunciation, the birth, the circumcision, and the manifestation of John and of Jesus are compared.

In non-Catholic exegesis the two chapters of the childhood Gospel of Luke are largely considered to be mythical, legendary tales. More correctly one would say that there is in these narratives a new manner of expression which has an earlier model in what are known as haggada. This was a favorite style of story telling in late Judaism, strongly attached to the word of the Bible, and in which the events recorded are explained theologically. The style has an edifying character; it seeks for the meaning of an event in which the earlier saving hand of God for Israel makes up the background. In Luke 1 and 2, happenings and persons in the Old Testament are seen as earlier forms (types) of those which happened to Jesus.

The understanding of the author is messianic; he wants to show that in Jesus all the promises of the old covenant and the historical saving works of God were fulfilled. The appearances of the angels are taken from the realm of the apocalyptic, where they play a great role (cf. the Book of Daniel). These angels are bearers of God's revelation; their task is to show that now the time of consummation has been made manifest. In Luke 1 and 2 we have the oldest Jewish-Christian theology, which is above all Christology, acknowledgment of Christ as the Messiah and the Son of God. Essentially these accounts have historical value, but they must not be taken literally in every detail.

With this understanding of Luke 1 and 2, the text of the annunciation pericope (1:26–38) can be explained. In the sixth month of the pregnancy of Elizabeth, mother of John the Baptist, whose birth was announced to his father Zechariah by the angel Gabriel (1:5–22), the same angel came to Nazareth, to a virgin named Mary. Nazareth was an unimportant town in Galilee. The virgin was betrothed to Joseph. Among the Jews the betrothal was already considered to be a marriage contract, but the bride remained for about a year in the house of her father before the bridegroom brought her over to his own house.

The angel came to Mary and greeted her with the words: "Rejoice, O highly favored one. The Lord is with you." In place of a name that is usually given in a greeting, we read here: favored one. In Greek, use of this verb form indicates that the blessing is not to follow after this: it has preceded the announcement of the angel. The words "The Lord is with you" are not to be taken as a wish; they are an expression of assurance of the nearness of God.

Mary was frightened by this approach; the fact that the angel greeted her left her speechless. The angel calmed her with the words that Jesus used so often to his disciples: "Do not be afraid!" There was no reason why she should be afraid; she had found favor with God. He had chosen her to be the mother of the Messiah; this is his free grace-giving that precedes the deed of God that will be accomplished in her.

Verses 30 to 35 make up the high point of the angel's message and explain the meaning of the angel's designation of Mary as the "highly favored one"—a designation that she will merit as the mother of the Messiah. "You shall conceive and bear a son and you must name him Jesus." This sentence is evidently formulated after Isaiah 7:14: "The virgin shall be with child, and bear a son, and shall name him Immanuel." Luke is saying that what had been given in the eighth century before Christ to the prophet as a sign of salvation is now entirely fulfilled in Mary. Only the name of the child is different. According to Isaiah it should be called Immanuel (God with us). Mary's Son should have the name Jesus (the Greek form of the Aramaic word Jeschua: God is salvation).

"He will be great and will be called the Son of the Most High." This is not to be understood in the sense of later dogmatic theology, God's Son of like nature. It means one chosen by God. From the first moment of his existence Jesus is Messiah. As such God will give him the throne of his forefather David. The promises of the angel are all in line with the expectations of the Messiah that are contained in the Old Testament. Through the prophet Nathan God had promised King David that he would bestow his throne on a son from his lineage and give him his kingdom: "I will make his royal throne secure forever. I will be a father to him and he a son to me" (2 Sam 7:13f). What is said here of Solomon, the angel now applies to Jesus: he will be great and be called the Son of the Most High; God will give him the throne of David and his kingdom will have no end.

That Mary should ask, after these powerful promises by the angel: "How can this be since I do not know man?" is understandable. Her question does not come from doubt about God's word; her doubt was not like that of Zechariah, the father of John, who doubted the promise that was given him and was therefore punished (Lk 1:18–20). She is asking rather because she should know how she must now respond in action. Should she at once begin married life with her betrothed one, or should she wait until the day of the wedding arrives? "Not to know man" means the same as not to have marital intercourse.

Many earlier interpreters understood Mary's question to mean that she had made an agreement or a vow of perpetual virginity. This could hardly be correct because in pre-Christian times, and especially among the Jews, celibacy and sterility were considered to be shameful. An appreciation of consecrated virginity among the followers of Jesus came only with Christianity. Modern exegesis has arrived at a much more likely solution: it does not deal with any actual question of Mary's asking. The author of the Gospel has her ask in this way in order to formulate the promise given by the angel more accurately and to show that we are dealing with a conception of divine origin, one that occurred without any action of a human father.

"Holy Spirit will come upon you and the power of the Most High will cover you." "Holy Ghost" (in Greek without the article) means the same as "power of the Most High," the creative power of God. There is here no mention of the third person of the Trinity; the thought is still along the lines of the Old Testament, of the spirit of God by which he governed the world and guided the destiny of the people of Israel.

In other places in the Bible we read of the spirit of God coming upon a person in order to express a sudden, powerful, effective intervention of God. The miracle of the fatherless conception of Jesus is the highest revelation of the creative freedom of God. The word "cover" or "overshadow" expresses the same creative procedure. The expression reminds us of a cloud that throws its shadow on someone. Thus we read in Exodus 40:35 that Moses could not enter the tent of meeting in the desert "because of the cloud that rested on it and because of the glory of Yahweh that filled the tabernacle."

Hence it is the purpose of the narrator to try to show that the divine sonship of Jesus and his holiness is founded in the source of his existence in God. This is shown in the words following immediately in the narrative: "And so the child will be holy and will be called the Son of God." Of the Baptist the angel says to Zechariah that even from his mother's womb he will be filled with the Holy Spirit (Lk 1:15). With Jesus the situation is different: creatively the Spirit will give him existence, and so determine his innermost being and make him holy. The evangelist gives in this way a theological basis for the holiness of Jesus. "Holy" is not to be understood here in an ethical sense; it means here the incorporation of the Holy Spirit in the world. In the ancient Creed that Paul cites in Romans 1:3f Jesus is "in the order of the spirit, the spirit that was in him; he was proclaimed Son of God in all his power through his resurrection from the dead." The institution of the Messiah as Son of God is associated here with his resurrection; in Luke's view it follows already with his conception.

Finally, in this dialogue with the angel, Mary gets another sign that she should believe his words: the pregnancy of Elizabeth in her old age. As she who had been considered sterile could become a mother, so God can also bring motherhood to one who is a virgin. "For nothing is impossible with God."

The story ends with the simple answer of Mary: "I am the handmaid of the Lord; let what you have said be done to me." The first part of the sentence is an expression of oriental self-depreciation (cf. 1 Sam 25:41; 2 Sam 9:6). Spoken here to God, however, it is an expression of deep religious devotion. The second part of the statement shows her agreement with what God had decreed for her. It expresses her surpassing devotion and religious reverence for God.

Two Old Testament forms of presentation are the bases for the story of the annunciation of Mary; biblical science in recent times has pointed these out in the scheme of annunciation (cf. Gen 17:15–19) and the scheme of vocation (cf. Jer 1:4–10). The author of our story has combined the two forms by taking the announcement of the birth, the naming, and the future life of the promised child along with the vocation call. The adoption of these forms found often in the Old Testament is proved by the fact that in Luke 1:26–38 he had no earlier model to follow in recording the dialogue between Mary and the angel. This obliges the author to give more attention to the person of Jesus; his nature and its mystery must be explained. Jesus is the Messiah, the Son of God, who is destined to eternal glory. This confession comes from the early Church. The author has clothed it in a story and put it back to the time of Jesus. The core statement of the whole section is found in verse 32; verses 34–37 develop and illustrate it. But it is very questionable whether we can infer from this that only verse 32, which professes Jesus' Sonship of God, is a doctrine of faith, while the teaching of the virginal conception by Mary is not. As will now be shown, the independent account in Matthew gives the same teaching as Luke, and states it more strongly.

THE ANCESTRY OF JESUS

"A genealogy of Jesus Christ, son of David, son of Abraham." Matthew begins his writing with this sentence, attaching to it a long list of names who represent the forefathers of Jesus. Certainly in making this list he does not give an accurately historical, unbroken family line, nor does he satisfy the pious curiosity of his readers. He is rather trying to demonstrate with this list the truth that Jesus is none other than the Messiah promised by God, as he is a descendant of Abraham and David. In other words, the evangelist wants to show the salvific importance of Jesus. He has composed this first chapter of his work himself, using, of course, the sources and the traditions available to him, as far as they suited his purpose.

It is easy to show that in Matthew 1 we do not have a family tree in the modern sense of the word. To show the line of descent the evangelist uses throughout the formula "A begot B." But this does not necessarily give the natural paternity in every case; sometimes the meaning is a substitute paternity, for example by adoption. By adoption of a strange child, that child comes into the line of descent of the adoptive father. If this adoptive father was a descendant of Abraham, the adopted son then carries on the line of promise to the patriarch Abraham. If the child is adopted by a descendant of David, he thereby gains title to the royal throne of David.

It is strange that we also meet names of women in the genealogical tree of David, and these not the great ancestral women like Sarah and Rebecca and Rachel; the ones given are heathens or sinners. Thus Tamar, the mother of Perez and Zerah (v 3), procured progeny by her father-in-law Judah in a very questionable way (Gen 13:38ff). Rahab, the low woman of Jericho, helped the scouts sent by Joshua (Jos 2) and was spared by the Israelites when they sacked the city. A pagan like Ruth, the Moabitess mentioned in verse 5, she was named as one of the ancestral women of David and of the Messiah. Besides these three women mentioned by name, Matthew also mentions Bathsheba, the mother of Solomon, but he does not give her name; he uses the paraphrase "the wife of Uriah" (v 6). In this he alludes to the adultery of David and the murder of Uriah (2 Sam 11:2–27). Mention of the four women indicates the main thought of the whole geneaology: the whole line of generations is directed toward the birth of the Messiah. What is sinful and devious and shunned by people cannot hinder the gracious choice of God; he does not avoid roundabout ways in order to achieve his end.

Though Matthew gives the names of women who do not belong to the genealogical tree of Jesus, he does omit three certified generations that the Old Testament gives, the kings Ahaziah, Joash, and Amaziah (cf. 1 Chr 3:11f), since all three worshiped idols; moreover they descended from Athaliah, the daughter of King Ahab of Israel (cf. 2 Chr 22:2–25, 27). By order of Yahweh the prophet Elijah had predicted the fall of the house of Ahab (cf. 1 Kgs 21:21). Hence Matthew leaves out the names of these bad kings in the list of the ancestors of the Messiah, and thereby shows that he was not concerned in having an unbroken line in the genealogy of the Messiah.

Verse 17 says that there are fourteen generations in each of the three divisions: from Abraham to David, then from David to the exile in Babylon, and from there to Christ. Actually there were many more. Only three generations are named (v 4) for the time of the captivity in Egypt; according to Exodus 12:40 this captivity lasted for four hundred and thirty years. For the time between Nahshon and David, which covered a period of at least two hundred and fifty years, only four generations are mentioned. Hence when the evangelist says that there were fourteen generations in each of the three periods he mentions, this cannot be an actual historical statement. For the first period he found a basis for the number of fourteen generations in the Old Testament (1 Chr 2:1–15). He sees this number as twice seven, and seven is the number for the perfect and the divine. With these numbers he wants to express the fact that God had watched over Israel and the kingdom of Judah in this way in order that these earthly

dominions reached their perfection and final conclusion in
Jesus. To express these thoughts with the help of numeri-
cal symbolism the evangelist had to renounce claim to an
exact genealogical list and had to be satisfied with an arti-
ficial and approximate one.

In verse 16 Matthew departs from the "A begot B"
scheme that he has been using for the whole list thus far
and says: "Jacob was the father of Joseph the husband of
Mary; of her was born Jesus who is called Christ." This is
probably the reading of the original source. Two other
readings are found in many manuscripts and provide later
corrections. In these formulations the author wishes to indicate that Jesus was not the natural son of Joseph even
though he was brought into the world by Joseph's lawful
wife Mary. Legally then Joseph was the father of Jesus and
Jesus was proved to be a rightful descendant of David.

The mother of the child is mentioned by name because
only she, without the cooperation of her spouse, gave life
to the child. The proper father of Jesus is specified by the
passive form of the verb: "of her was born." We have a case
here of the use of what is called the theological or divine
passive, commonly used in those times by the Jews to paraphrase the action of God without having to express his
name.

But Matthew is not satisfied with this roundabout sig-
nification. In an extended footnote to verse 16 he explains
explicitly how the begetting of Jesus came about (vv 18–25).
This section gives theological basis for the proper statements of verse 16: Jesus was the son of Joseph only in a
figurative sense; in the proper sense he is the son of God.
The author puts this theological teaching in the form of a
story in which he incidentally reveals his minor interest in
historical details. About the time and place of the event he
makes no assertions (he brings this up only later, in 2:1, and

there very briefly), and he does not introduce us properly
to the persons who are participating. Evidently he could assume that his readers knew about these things already.

He says only: "His mother Mary was betrothed to Joseph; but before they came to live together she was found
to be with child." We are not told who discovered the pregnancy of Mary. Possibly it was Joseph himself. The evangelist's phrase "through the Holy Spirit" presumes that in
what the angel tells Joseph in verse 20.

The evangelist describes the reaction of Joseph on
learning of Mary's pregnancy in these words: "Her husband Joseph, being a man of honor and wanting to spare
her publicity, decided to divorce her informally." There is
still much doubt about the motive for this decision. The
"honor" of Joseph was not a kind of rigid legalism which
would require that Mary be handed over to be executed for
adultery according to the law of Leviticus 20:10. The word
"honor" in this case may well be taken to mean "kindness,
mercy."

Therefore he wanted to give her a bill of divorce in
which the grounds for the separation need not be mentioned. In this way Mary could return to her parental home
and need not have any fear of being punished as an adulter-
ess. Another explanation says that Joseph knew of the divine origin of her pregnancy. He wanted to let her go out of
a spirit of reverence because he believed that he no longer
had any claim on her after God had laid his hand on her.

According to Matthew, an angel of the Lord put an end
to Joseph's doubts in a dream; this is a paraphrase to state
that there was actual intervention of God in which his will
was made known. Joseph's being addressed as "Son of
David" indicates that Jesus received the sonship of David
from Joseph; but divine sonship comes to him only from
God.

Verse 21 is made up of two texts from the Old Testament. In Isaiah 7:14 we read: "The maiden is with child and will soon give birth to a son whom she will call Immanuel (God with us)" (Matthew replaces only the word "Immanuel" with "Jesus"). In Ps Psalm 130:8 we read: "It is he who redeems Israel from all their sins" (instead of "Israel" the evangelist here says "his people"). What the psalm says of Yahweh Matthew transfers to the child of Mary. The psalm verse explains the name of Jesus: Yahweh is salvation. In New Testament times the meaning of the name was taken from the verbs "to save, to redeem," and hence the word Jesus was understood in the sense of "Savior, Redeemer." Joseph should give the child of Mary this name for the reason that the child will heal his people from their sins—he will save them.

Verses 22 and 23 are a reflection-citation; that is, Matthew cites Isaiah 7:14 and reflects on its fulfillment in the life of Jesus. The text belongs to one of the difficult places in the writings of the prophets. And thereby with the evangelist we meet the difficulty in the word "Immanuel." If the child of Mary was known already in the Old Testament as "God with us," it is a reference to him as Son of God, as one conceived by the Holy Ghost. It gives us a scriptural proof of Christ which was not valid for the Jews of that time since the text was not generally understood as a messianic one. Moreover, in the original text the reference is not to a virgin; it uses the word that means a young woman and one who could be married. It was only in the Greek translation that the Hebrew word of the Old Testament *alma* was translated as *parthenos* (virgin).

In the following two verses (24f) Matthew takes up an Old Testament formula which is often used when there is talk of carrying out the commands of God. He wants to show that Joseph carried out the divine command given him by the angel exactly as he was told. He brought Mary home with him, which means he celebrated the marriage with her and gave her child the name after he was born. The evangelist explains that the text "The virgin will bear a son" was completely fulfilled with the statement by saying: "He (Joseph) had not had intercourse with her when she bore a son." It is mistaken to conclude from this statement that Joseph begot other children by Mary after the birth of Jesus. The Gospel says nothing about this.

As we have seen, the genealogical tree of Jesus wishes to show that he was the son of Abraham and David. Matthew goes a step further in verses 18–25 and shows that the child of Mary is the true Son of God because he was conceived without the participation of a human father through a miraculous intervention of God in the womb of a virgin. Hence we have here an unequivocal witness for the virgin motherhood of Mary. But the evangelist does not derive the "proof" for this belief from the text of Isaiah 7:14. He cites it only as confirmation of an already existent ancient tradition. This tradition, which is also found in Luke, is not a creation of theological speculation. The great theologians of the New Testament, Paul, John, and the author of the Letter to the Hebrews, do not speak of it. Apparently already from the beginning of Christianity it was held as a teaching closely connected with the mystery of the incarnation.

THE BIRTH OF JESUS

The verses 2:1–14 make up, without doubt, the high point of Luke's childhood Gospel. He tells us of the actual good news of the birth of Jesus and the circumstances around it. In his plain and concise style his writing seems to be in palpable contrast to the meaning of the events he is telling of. We are told of the birth of the Son of God on earth without any poetic or edifying embellishments.

Closer study is required before one observes that this is not a simple historical report, and much less an edifying legend, aimed at awakening pious sentiments in the reader. There is in this text a special art of narration which has earlier instances in the Old Testament. An historical event is put into words and at the same time it is explained theologically and credibly. The story is not a simple narrative; it is also proclamation and confession. There are two parts to the story: the birth of Jesus (vv 1–7) and the announcement to the shepherds (vv 8–14).

The evangelist tries to tie the salvation event of the birth of Jesus into world history in the first verse. Caesar Augustus issued a decree that a census of the whole world should be taken. The purpose of this was to get more complete tax lists, giving information about taxable persons and property. All were to state where they had landed property along with their names on the list.

Historians have gotten many headaches over this notice that Luke gives here. Nothing is known about any such general decree; there are records of some local ones that went out. In the years 10 to 9 B.C. such a tax listing was made in Egypt; a similar one took place in Gaul in 9 B.C. One such is known to have been issued for Palestine for the years 6 to 7 A.D.; it was carried out by the Roman procurator in Syria, Quirinus. It cannot be proved that this same official ordered an earlier one in this same country; it is possible that there was such an earlier tax listing made.

Up to this day no satisfactory solution has been reached to explain these difficulties. At best it can be said that we are dealing with a remark of the author that is not chronologically accurate; he was writing some decades after the event. It is certain that the author does want to demonstrate the worldwide importance of the birth of Jesus when he calls attention to Caesar Augustus. Jesus is not only the Messiah awaited by the Jews; he is the Savior of the whole world.

That Joseph would want to take Mary along to Bethlehem is easy to understand: she was pregnant and he did not want to leave her alone at home in Nazareth. In any case we would expect that this journey, which took about four days (the distance between Nazareth and Bethlehem is about eighty-five miles), was not made in the very last days of Mary's confinement, else it would have been too difficult for Mary. Mary is still called the "betrothed" of Joseph, even though in the interval he had brought her to his home and she was his wife.

The time for her delivery came during their stay in Bethlehem, "and she gave birth to a son, her first-born." The event could not have been more simply told. It does not follow from the description of Jesus as first-born that Mary had other children later. A Jewish sepulchral inscription dating from the year 5 B.C. honors a young mother who died in the birth of her first-born child. "First-born" means the same as "dedicated to God," for according to Exodus 13:12 every first-born male was to be consecrated to God.

Mary wrapped the child in swaddling clothes. This only says that Jesus was a wrapped child—that is, in keeping with the customs of those times, a newborn child was kept closely wrapped to keep his limbs straight. She laid him in a crib, a feeding trough for cattle. As a reason for the use of such a different kind of cradle, Luke says that it was because there was no room for them in the inn. It is disputed whether this means a public inn (would a small place like Bethlehem have one?) or some private dwelling:

this can also be understood from the words the evangelist uses. This would mean that no suitable shelter had been found for the imminent birth.

Hence we suppose that Jesus came into the world in an empty stable or in a cave that served as a stable. Emperor Constantine actually built a church over such a cave in the fourth century, and in so doing he seems to have followed some local tradition. What is remarkable and inspiring about this birth is that it is so ordinary. Like every other child, Jesus was wrapped in swaddling clothes; he was a true child of man with a proper human body.

The swaddled child in the feed-trough is something of a paradox. It seems absurd that this should be regarded as some kind of special sign: this is what verse 12 says. The interpretation that this is something unusual comes from the second part of the pericope (vv 8–14), where there is help of many biblical references in the style of an Old Testament story.

A divine revelation came to the shepherds tending their flocks under the skies in the night watch. In the Old Testament shepherds have an important role in reference to the Messiah. David pastured his sheep in the meadows of Bethlehem and rose from being a shepherd to become king of Israel. Only in later times were shepherds regarded as despised and dishonorable people. Certainly, however, they were poor and belonged to the lower strata of the people. To these poor folk the good news was first made manifest. An angel of the Lord came to them and the heavenly light of the Lord shone on them. In the Old Testament such a visible illumination always accompanies an apparition of God. The amazement of the shepherds is the natural reaction to receiving the divine revelation. The angel reassures them that now is not the time for fear, since a

great joy has come to them. "Today in the town of David a
Savior has been born to you; he is Christ the Lord."

"Today": salvation is seen as something already present.
It became present in the birth of Jesus. To the child in the
crib the angel gives three significant titles. He is *Savior,* a
term reserved only to God in the New Testament (cf. Lk
1:47) and his Messiah (Acts 5:31; Jn 4:42). In the older Gospels of Mark and Matthew we do not find these terms used.
But in the pagan world of Luke, some gods and the Roman
emperor were given the titles of "Soter" (which means savior). Luke wants them to be replaced by the one true Savior,
Jesus. The word "Soter" is found some five hundred and
thirty times in the Greek translation of the Old Testament as
a translation of the divine name Yahweh. Hence it is quite
probable that Luke wants the word to be understood as the
divine predicate: Jesus is the divine Savior.

The second title is *Messiah,* which means Christ, the
anointed One. This is what the prophets called the one
coming to bring salvation. The name of highest honor is
last, the *Lord,* Kyrios. Here the evangelist almost certainly
wishes to put Jesus equal to God. This is so extraordinary
that efforts were made to put in another word as the original reading; this was the expression "the anointed One of
the Lord." But the much better-attested expression is the
Messiah, the Lord. "Kyrios" is the most common word by
far for the name of God in the Greek Bible. There is no
more noble name for the child in the crib than to call him
Kyrios.

The shepherds were given a sign to verify the angel's
message: they would see a child lying in a crib and wrapped
in swaddling clothes. A more absurd sign could hardly be
imagined: a helpless child in a feed-trough was the sign of
the coming of God on earth! In order that the shepherds

should have no doubts about the greatness of the child there suddenly appeared a great choir of other angels. A heavenly host was there with the angel of proclamation, who gave glorious witness in the words: "Honored be God in the highest, and on earth peace to the people of his grace." This is one translation that has been given; the most common version is: Glory to God in the highest, and on earth peace to men of good will. The two-part sentence is not considered to be a wish (let there be glory); it is rather a statement that through the incarnation of the Son of God, God *is* truly honored. The second half of the sentence is also a statement: now there is peace on earth among the people.

The people are more definitely described as those of the divine grace, that is, those to whom God has given his grace. The word that is used in the original text is *eudokia,* which now and then means a human attribute; mostly though it means God-given grace. The translation that Luther gives, which was taken over by the churches of the Reformation, also rests on a false reading. It breaks the sentence into three parts: Glory to God in the heights and peace on earth, to men a good will. The oldest and best manuscripts read: men of good will.

What is the meaning of this short hymn? Through the birth of the Son of God, God glorifies himself. Jesus is the perfect revelation of God; his birth as a child of mankind makes God's deepest being, his love, known to us. "In the highest" ratifies this honoring: to the angels of heaven God shows his power and his mercy. "Peace on earth" here does not mean a good understanding, or the undisturbed living together of individuals and nations. The word translated as "peace" is the Hebrew word *shalom,* the attribute of one who brings salvation. For mankind has been made sharer in divine salvation and heavenly grace; we have obtained forgiveness of sin through the birth of Jesus. This salvation has not been promised for some distant future; it is as actual as the glorification of God in heaven and the joy of the shepherds.

This sharing of salvation by all mankind is not meant to be restricted by the phrase "to the people of grace"; it does not limit salvation to some definite group to whom God gives his special good will. No, all people are "people of grace"; in Christ all are called to salvation. Hence that second member of the sentence does not add more meaning to it than the first part: God is glorified in the very fact that he has given all mankind salvation.

We can say, then, that Luke 2:14 is the high point of the revelation of Christ in the childhood Gospel. In this verse God has made known to the early Church the mystery of his Son as understandably as possible. Here there is a profound light shed on what the Apostles' Creed expresses in the concise phrase: "born of the Virgin Mary." As externals go the birth of Jesus in the stable at Bethlehem differs little from the birth of every human child. But it is still infinitely more: in it God gives the world his Son, through whom he has brought salvation close to all mankind and made it attainable for all.

For those who understand this, the question whether this disclosure came about literally in the way Luke tells us is secondary; whether there was actually an angelic host that sang is not of prime importance. Many modern interpreters consider these only as images; in fact many consider the whole section, 2:8–14, to be a creation of the early Church in which its faith in the divinity of the child of Bethlehem was expressed. Such an interpretation does not, in any case, change anything that is essential in the Christmas message that has been given its unique character to this section of the childhood Gospel of Luke.

IV
SUFFERED UNDER PONTIUS PILATE, WAS CRUCIFIED, DIED, AND WAS BURIED, DESCENDED INTO THE KINGDOM OF THE DEAD

The fourth article of the apostolic symbol encompasses the profession of the passion of Jesus in five statements: he suffered, he was crucified, he died, he was buried, and he descended into hell. No other statement of faith is so particularly expressed in the Gospels as the passion and death of Jesus. All four Gospels tell us of it. Apparently in early Christianity a strong need was felt for a comprehensive report of these events. Already in the first decade after the death of Jesus such a report had to be written down in the founding community in Jerusalem. This was taken over with only slight changes by Mark and incorporated in his Gospel. To deal with all or even with only the most important texts in the Gospels that tell of the suffering and death of Jesus would go beyond the limits of our study here. We will take up only a few that require a special explanation.

SUFFERED UNDER PONTIUS PILATE

That the name of the Roman prefect who condemned Jesus to death should be mentioned in the symbol may appear surprising. Surely, however, this locates the point in time historically in which the event took place. Pilate was the Roman governor in Judea and Samaria in the years 26 to 36. In this office he, and only he, was empowered to impose the death penalty. For this reason the Jewish mob handed Jesus over to Pilate as a notorious blasphemer whom they found guilty of the death penalty. But when they found the Roman official unwilling to be persuaded of this on the basis of such a charge, they resorted to representing him as a political rebel against the Roman imperial power (Lk 23:2). Pilate recognized the political inoffensiveness of Jesus and sought to dismiss the charges against him. But the excited crowd put him under pressure. In order to appease them he had Jesus scourged; this, however, did not achieve his purpose. What was worse, he brought up a convicted offender and had him placed beside Jesus, and then let the crowd choose which of the two should be given freedom. In this indirect way he gave the impression that Jesus also had earned the death penalty. Finally he gave in to the rabble and condemned Jesus to death by crucifixion.

The Synoptics, especially Matthew and Luke, try as far as possible to absolve Pilate from blame for the death of Jesus; they put the blame on the Jewish high council. The fourth evangelist is especially taken up with the role of Pilate in the condemnation of Jesus (Jn 18:28—19:16). He is also convinced of the innocence of Pilate, as he explicitly says three times. But finally he yields to the pressure of the Jews and, against his better judgment, pronounces the death sentence; thereby he makes himself guilty of the murder of an innocent person. However, in John's view, the Jews bear the main burden of guilt for the death of Jesus; Pilate is, at the same time, only the instrument and is indeed thereby guilty of cooperation in the offense.

CRUCIFIED

That Jesus suffered death by crucifixion is explicitly stated by all the evangelists and elsewhere in the New Testament. At the time when Jesus lived, execution by crucifixion was the most shameful form of capital punishment, reserved for slaves and rebels. In one of his orations, the Roman author Cicero is defending an official who had been accused of having Roman citizens crucified, and he says: "The idea of the cross should be foreign not only to the physical bodies of Roman citizens, but also to their thoughts, to their eyes, their ears." Among respectable people there should not even be mention of such a disgraceful manner of death. For Christian missionaries it was a difficult task to make comprehensible to their audiences why Jesus, who was honored by his followers as a sinless man and as the Son of God, should have to suffer such a death.

The evangelists also saw the necessity of making the crucifixion of Jesus understandable to their readers. It is for this reason that they give such detail to the trial of Jesus. The enemies of Jesus could bring the Roman judge to pronounce the death sentence only by bringing in false witnesses who accused him of rebellion.

Pilate had a sign put on the cross to indicate the reason for the execution; it was written in the three languages of the country: Hebrew, Latin, and Greek, and read: Jesus of Nazareth, the King of the Jews (Jn 19:19). No doubt he wished to irritate the high priests and their followers by doing this. They had refused to accept Jesus as their King (Jn 19:15). Now the procurator had him crucified, labeled as the King of the Jews, and given a place of honor between two robbers. The Jews noticed this subtlety of the procurator and demanded that he should change the inscription to indicate simply that Jesus *said* he was the King of the

Jews. But Pilate would not agree to this. He wanted the
high priests to know that objections of a political kind
against Rome would bring the same result to them as they
had for Jesus. Since they had refused to accept Jesus as
King (Jn 19:15) and acknowledged Caesar as their ruler,
Pilate acceded to their wishes because of their fidelity to the
emperor.

DIED AND WAS BURIED

That in a profession of faith, otherwise so concisely
formulated, the death of Jesus should be paraphrased with
three expressions is extraordinary: he was crucified, died,
and was buried. Apparently this was done to establish the
fact of the death of Jesus as absolutely certain. This could
have been done to oppose the heresy of docetism, which
stated that Jesus had only an imaginary body, and hence
could not really have been killed. Against this view the
Christians maintained that Jesus actually died on the cross,
and his dead body was laid in a tomb.

The evangelists give witness to the reality of the death
of Jesus in various ways. Mark tells us (15:42ff) that a Jewish councillor, Joseph of Arimathea, asked for the body of
Jesus so that he could bury it. Ordinarily the bodies of people who were executed were not released to their relatives;
they were thrown into a common grave. Pilate was surprised when he heard that Jesus was already dead. Those
who were crucified generally hung for hours, even days, on
the cross until they finally died of suffocation. Hence he
first got a report from the centurion in charge of the execution squad, who assured him that Jesus was dead; then
he gave Joseph the right to remove the body.

John also tells of this (19:31ff). The bodies of the three

who had been executed had to be removed from their crosses on the same day so that they would not be hanging there on the sabbath. Apparently the two thieves were still alive; therefore the soldiers broke their legs in order to hasten death. But Jesus was already dead. In order to be absolutely sure of this, and not to let themselves be deceived by appearances, one of the soldiers pierced the side of Jesus in the region of his heart; in that way he would give him the death stroke, if that was necessary. John says particularly that water and blood flowed from the heart wound. Perhaps his intention in giving this remark is to emphasize the actual death of a real man in order to oppose the opinion of the docetists. But almost certainly there is further significance and higher purpose in the statement: he is referring to baptism and the Eucharist. This does not exclude the immediate sense of the words: Jesus actually died on the cross.

The addition to the statement in the profession of faith also strives to stress this truth: *he was buried.* It is interesting that this addition is found already in the oldest formula of faith in the New Testament, which was written some thirty years earlier by the apostle Paul around the year 55, and given in 1 Corinthians 15:4. Paul is also stressing the reality of the death of Jesus.

Where the last statement of the fourth article adds that *he descended into hell,* the intention is again to exclude the idea of an apparent death. To go down into "sheol," into the underworld, is a reference to the Old Testament region, the final place of separation of those who have departed this earthly life.

WHY DID JESUS DIE ON THE CROSS?

Already in the New Testament we find efforts to explain somehow the inexplicable fact of the death of Jesus on the cross to the readers. John says (5:16ff) that there are two main reasons why the Jews wanted to have Jesus executed: because he violated the law of the sabbath, and thereby the Mosaic law, and because he made himself equal to God. The same law, however, gives the punishment for violation of the sabbath and for blasphemy to be by stoning to death. Moreover, these external reasons actually do not apply to Jesus. He did not reject the Mosaic law as such; he only rejected the rabbinic interpretation of it and carried its application back to the original will of God. Likewise his claim to equality with God was not blasphemy against God since he was telling the truth.

The oldest communities in Palestine saw the fate of their ancient prophets repeated in the shameful death of Jesus. As their prophets had been hounded and killed, so Jesus also had to suffer the same fate. In a cry of lamentation to the scribes and Pharisees we read: "Woe to you . . . you hypocrites! You build up the tombs of the prophets and engrave the monuments of the just; if we had lived in our fathers' times, you say, we would never have been guilty of the death of the prophets. In this you say yourselves that you are the sons of murderers of the prophets. . . . Now behold, I am sending you prophets and wise men and men of learning; some of them you will put to death and even crucify them; others you will scourge in your synagogues and persecute them from city to city" (Mt 23:29–31, 34).

The earthly Jesus could hardly have spoken these prophetic words of judgment; they were probably written by a Christian prophet and were directed at the Pharisees of his own time, who considered themselves to be better than their fathers. They acknowledged the prophetic words from the past without making themselves open to prophetic activity in the present. In any case the text shows that the fate of Jesus was seen in the same light as that of the ancient prophets.

Mark's Gospel speaks often of the divine "necessity" of the death of Jesus—for example, in the first announcement of the coming passion: "And now he began to make it known to them that the Son of Man *must* be ill-treated and be rejected by the elders and the chief priests and scribes; he would be put to death and would rise again in three days" (Mk 8:31). Fulfillment of the will of God is seen in the passion and death of Jesus. What seems externally to be a human decision is actually divine history. The enemies of Jesus are only the instruments by which this is achieved.

Especially notable is the fulfillment of Old Testament Scriptures in the death of Jesus. The risen Savior said to the two disciples at Emmaus: "Did not the Messiah have to suffer all this in order to enter into his glory?" (Lk 24:26). The evangelists allude to this again and again: Jesus had to suffer this and that in order that the Scriptures would be fulfilled (cf. Mt 26:56; Jn 19:28, 36f); indeed, they often give details of the passion in the words of the Old Testament (cf. Mt 27:35 = Ps 22:19; Lk 23:46 = Ps 31:6).

Very early the death of Jesus was explained as atonement for mankind and for the sins of the people. We find this already in the account of the Last Supper of Jesus with his disciples. As he gives them the chalice he says: "This is my blood, the blood of the covenant, which shall be poured out for many" (Mk 14:24); Matthew, in the parallel text, adds explicitly: "for the remission of sins" (26:28). Luke gives us the supper-words of Jesus in this way: "This is my body which is to be given for you" (Lk 22:19).

Already in the ancient form of profession of faith that Paul gives us in 1 Corinthians 15:3 we read: "As the Scriptures had fortold: Christ died for our sins." This and similar "for-us" expressions mean that in his death Jesus suffered in our place and in that way made atonement for the sins of mankind.

In John's Gospel the death of Jesus on the cross is no longer seen as the terrible happening that it was; rather, it is described as a victory over the world and the triumphal return of Jesus to the Father. Where there is mention of the "raising" of Jesus on the cross there is a twofold meaning: it is not only the nailing and the erection of the cross; it is also the glorification of Jesus and the establishment of his reign. As we read in John 12:32: "Yes, if only I am lifted up from the earth, I will attract all to myself."

All these interpretations of the death of Jesus on the cross that we find in the New Testament still have their value today. But they do not give the most profound reason why Jesus died on the cross. This reason we find touched on particularly in John's Gospel—for instance in 3:16: "God so loved the world that he gave up his only-begotten Son, so that those who believe in him may not perish, but have eternal life." This "giving-up" refers first of all to the sending of the Son into the world. Jesus is the gift of God to mankind. But his sacrificial death is also understood as the highest proof of God's love for us. In other texts, where there is mention of this sacrifice, the meaning is unequivocally the way it was carried out in death. In fact, it seems that Jesus himself used this expression.

In order to impress on his disciples that they were called to serve others, and not to be served by them, he refers to his own conduct: "So it is that the Son of Man did not come to let himself be served; he came to serve others and to give his life as a ransom for the lives of many" (Mk

10:45). Granted that there is question of the authenticity of this verse, it is still quite conceivable that Jesus did consider the possibility of a violent death. And he could find an explanation of this fate in the prophecy of Isaiah, who writes of the servant of God: "And yet he bore our sufferings and carried our miseries . . . he was pierced through for our offenses and crushed for our sins" (53:4f). Hence the idea of crucifixion as atonement for sin may be referred to him, even though the statement of it was first made in final form after his resurrection.

While the love of God for mankind brings us the most profound reason for handing over his Son in death of atonement, it must also be said that Jesus took death on himself from the same motive. In his account of the Last Supper, the fourth evangelist says: "This is my commandment, that you should love one another, as I have loved you. There is no greater love than this, that one should lay down his life for his friends" (Jn 15:12f). In the word-picture of the good shepherd, we read: "Therefore the Father loves me because I lay down my life in order to take it up again afterward. No one takes it from me; I lay it down of my own accord" (Jn 10:17f). These words also may be of later composition, but the self-sacrifice of Jesus in death because of his love for us belongs to the strongest convictions of the apostle Paul: "I have been crucified with Christ, and yet I am alive; or rather, not I; it is Christ that lives in me. I am living here and now this mortal life, but my real life is the faith I have in the Son of God who loved me and gave himself for me" (Gal 2:19f).

V
ON THE THIRD DAY
HE ROSE FROM THE DEAD

In the New Testament, faith in the resurrection of Jesus from the dead is attested in many ways. The oldest testimony is found in 1 Corinthians 15:4f: "He rose again on the third day, as the Scriptures foretold, and appeared first to Cephas, and then to the twelve." In opposition to certain Corinthians who doubted the general resurrection of mankind or else considered this to be something superfluous, Paul appeals to an old profession of faith in the resurrection of Jesus from the dead in order to show the firm bond of faith in the Savior's resurrection with the faith in resurrection of the Christian. This good news, as Paul himself tells us, he received when he became a Christian; it goes back to thirty years before. Soon after the death of Jesus there must have been a fixed form of profession of faith: in order to be saved one needed to adhere to it in every word (cf. 1 Cor 15:2). The first part of this formula was included in the apostolic Creed, with this difference—that it does not read "he was raised," as Paul puts it, but "he rose from the dead," hence that he returned by his own divine power.

The added statement "on the third day" is put in to fix the time of the resurrection. In the early Church this was considered an event to be fixed in time and history. We find the expression in Luke 24:21. There the disciples at Emmaus say to Jesus who was walking incognito with them:

"And also, this is the third day since it all happened" (meaning the execution of Jesus). In other places in the Gospels there are similar expressions: "after three days" (Mk 8:31), or even: the Son of Man will be three days and three nights in the heart of the earth (Mt 12:40). Since this is only an approximate expression, it can well be understood as "a couple of days." According to oriental customs, a stay up to three days is only a short stay, while one of four days is a lengthy one. The fifth article of faith as we have it in the symbol means that Jesus was dead for only a short time, not forever. In these estimations of time almost certainly an historical recollection is maintained, either of the discovery of the empty grave or of the first apparition of the risen Savior.

If we ask ourselves what we find in the Gospels about this article of faith, we can say that all four of the evangelists tell of it. In Mark's Gospel, particularly in the part written by the evangelist himself (16:9–20 is a later addition), there is only a single sentence telling of it: an angel talks to the women who had come to the grave: "He is risen; he is not here" (16:6). Matthew likewise tells of this message of the angel, and adds mention of the appearance of Jesus to the women, and also of an appearance to eleven disciples in Galilee. Luke likewise tells of the angel's message, and adds to it the account of the appearance of Jesus to the disciples at Emmaus, along with two other appearances: to Peter, and to the eleven apostles. Finally John tells of an appearance of the risen One to Mary Magdalene and of two further appearances to the disciples in Jerusalem; in the supplementary Chapter 21 there is mention of still another appearance to seven disciples on the Lake of Gennesareth. We cannot discuss all these texts here; it will be sufficient if we speak of two facts: the discovery of the empty tomb, and the appearances of Jesus as witnessing the resurrection.

THE DISCOVERY OF THE EMPTY TOMB

The Easter accounts of the Gospels contain elements that cannot all be brought into agreement. For this reason they are often seen as statements historically unreliable or else as late legends. Can we say this then of the accounts of the discovery of the empty grave?

The earliest evangelist Mark tells (16:1–8) of three women among the followers of Jesus who, after the sabbath ended, bought oil to use in anointing the body of Jesus. On the first day of the week (in the Christian view, on Easter Sunday) they went very early to his grave. Mark lists the same women (15:40) as witnesses of the death of Jesus, and two of them (15:47) as eye-witnesses also of his grave. We should not take the anointing of the body of Jesus as a form of embalming (such a custom was unknown among Jews of that time); it was merely application of fragrant oil to take away the odor of corruption. Possibly on Good Friday evening the anointing of the body was left undone; at least Mark does not mention that it was done then. In any case, the women wanted to enter the place of burial, which was probably a cave that had been cut into the rock. On the way to the grave they were worried about how they would be able to roll away the heavy stone that covered the entrance to the burial place. But as they approached the place they saw that the stone had already been moved away and they would not have to be concerned about that difficulty.

Matthew elaborates the scene somewhat: there was a strong earthquake, and an angel came from heaven and moved away the stone and sat on it (28:2). But the evangelist does not tell us whether Jesus rose from the grave when it was closed or when it was open. He gives as little description of the actual events of the resurrection as Mark does.

On entering the burial chamber the women saw a young man sitting there to the right side, clad in a white garment. They recognized him as a person belonging to the heavenly world. His seat toward the right side indicated that he was bringing good news. According to Matthew 28:3 his appearance was like lightning and his clothing white as snow. According to Luke 24:4 the women saw two men clad in glowing garments. From the accepted law, two men could be considered to be confirming legal witnesses. The frightening of the women at the sight of the angel at the grave corresponded to the reaction of people in the Old Testament when they experienced the appearance of an angel. And the words that the angel said—"Have no fear!" (Mt 28:5)—are also found in Old Testament apparitions of heavenly beings. The angel (Mk 16:6) sees the coming of the women as a search for the crucified Jesus. The word "to search" does not fit the situation well: the women already knew where Jesus was buried. The angel is simply leading up to the following statement: "He is risen; he is not here."

A more accurate translation would be: He has been awakened. We have here what is called a theological passive: it describes a divine activity. Hence the sentence means: God has awakened him. The expression used in the Greek for awakening or resuscitating can also mean waking from sleep. Applied here to the crucified Jesus it means the undescribable event: he has conquered death. As one who has been raised up he is no longer in the grave. Only after giving this information does the angel bring up mention of the empty grave. The empty burial place is really not the source of the Easter-faith of the women: it is only a symbol of it, to help them to understand the Easter message and to confirm it. Perhaps one can say that the sentence "See, here is the place where they laid him" is telling us that the earliest community in Jerusalem already had a special devotion to the holy sepulchre.

The angel then told the women that they should go to the disciples, and particularly to Peter, to bring them the news of the resurrection. It is true that in Mark 14:50 we read that the disciples fled when Jesus was taken into custody; Mark does not tell us where they went, but apparently it was not to their homes in Galilee. For the statement here (16:7) that says, "He is going before you into Galilee; there you shall see him," assumes that they are still staying in Jerusalem and are not yet gone. The further remark "as he has told you" refers to 14:28. There at the Last Supper Jesus said to his disciples: "I will go on before you into Galilee when I have risen from the dead."

The evangelist does not tell us anything about the disappearance of the angel; he only says that the women went off quickly "trembling and awe-struck, out of fear." The cause of this terror was not simply the discovery of the empty tomb; most of all they were awestruck by the meeting with the angel and the news of the resurrection. As Mark says, it was out of fear that they told no one else about what they had seen and heard at the grave.

With this remark the original version of Mark's Gospel ends. The following verses, 9 through 20, that we have in our editions were added only much later by another hand. At first sight it is difficult to understand why Mark does not tell us of a meeting of the risen Christ with the disciples. It is misleading to assume that the original ending of the Gospel had gotten lost or that it was replaced by the present one. Nearly all exegetes today maintain that the evangelist ended his writing with the words "for they were afraid." The news of the resurrection has already been given in what he had written before; now the reader is asked what position he should take regarding it.

Matthew took over the material that Mark used, but added to it some details from other traditions. In an effort to counteract a false interpretation that had been given about the empty tomb (that the disciples had opened the grave and removed the body of Jesus), he added the scene of the guards that had been sent to the tomb (27:62–66). This says that on the day after the death of Jesus the high priests and the Pharisees went to Pilate and asked that a guard detail be sent to the grave, so that the disciples of Jesus could not steal his body and then spread a report among the people that he had risen from the dead. Pilate appointed these watchmen for them, and also ordered that the entrance to the tomb should be sealed.

Accordingly the resurrection of Jesus is presented as a miraculous liberation. There was a great earthquake; an angel rolled the stone away from the entrance to the grave and sat down on it. The fear of the watchmen is also mentioned: they fell to the ground, as if struck dead. In that way they would be excluded from consideration as witnesses for the resurrection message. There is some interesting irony here that the evangelist wants to share with us: the watchmen went to the high priests and told them *everything* that had happened, but they had really not seen anything. As we see, Matthew deals rather freely with the materials of tradition available to him. Apparently his interest is more in a theological and apologetic interpretation than in an historical presentation of the event.

Luke does not give an historical report either, and he does not contribute any new or historically-reliable details to Mark's account, except to say that Peter inspected the empty grave. Luke does not accept the witness of the women (cf. 24:11: the apostles considered their report to be gossip and refused to believe it). He strengthens the authority of the angel's revelation (two men appeared, not just one). They do indeed announce the Easter message, but they interpret the death of Jesus mainly in a theological way: the Son of Man had to be handed over to sinners and be crucified, and to rise again on the third day (24:7).

Concerning the tradition of the empty grave it can certainly be said that it is older than our Gospels. It is unusual that women should discover the empty tomb, because in those times among the Jews women had no function as witnesses; their reports were considered to be questionable. Hence there is cause to accept this as an actual detail that goes back to an historical memorandum and is not something that was later fabricated in order to make the resurrection more credible. The fact of the empty grave was not disputed by the enemies of Jesus, though it was understood in a different way. The report of the resurrection could not have been maintained for one day in Jerusalem if it could have been shown that there was a tomb in which his body still lay. The finding of the empty tomb was, moreover, not represented as the source of Easter faith in the Gospels, nor was it used as a proof of the resurrection. It was only in the nineteenth century that the importance of the empty tomb became overrated in Catholic theology.

Concerning the angel at the tomb, there are three possible explanations:

1. A supernatural being actually appeared to the women and announced the Easter message to them. In this case the flight of the women is understandable, though their silence is not. Since the Old Testament pictures the entry of Yahweh through the appearance of an angel, the angel at the grave can also be simply a means of manifestation, a representation through which an event is interpreted.

2. The women discovered the empty grave on Easter morning, and thereby received from God a supernatural enlightenment: Jesus is actually risen. Thereby they felt required to share their discovery with the apostles. Later this interior discernment was reported as the message of an angel. In this explanation the flight and the silence of the women are not to be thought of as actual happenings. They are to be explained from the situation of the Church: in this way the extraordinary nature of the Easter message was shown and at the same time an effort was made to explain why so much remained hidden.

3. The women discovered the opened grave and were confused and surprised by it. The disciples had returned to Galilee, and there the risen One had appeared to them. The news "He has risen" spread from Galilee to Jerusalem and was there connected with the tradition of the empty grave. The proclamation "He has risen" counted as a revelation of God, and rightly so, since it had its origin in the appearance of Jesus. It was represented as a form of angelic apparition in order to stress the fact that the discovery of the empty grave is not an invention of the women: it is the revelation of God.

Every one of these three explanations has some probability but does not solve all the difficulties. In any case they show that the appearances of the angel at the grave of Jesus are not to be taken absolutely literally. But this does not bring the meaning of the Easter message into question.

In John's Gospel, which was composed around the

year 100 after Christ, we find an account (20:1–10) of the discovery of the empty tomb which agrees on many points with that of Mark, but also contains much that is proper to this later evangelist. It shows, moreover, that the discovery of the empty tomb was spoken of very early among the disciples and that it has come down to us in several different traditions.

According to John, Mary Magdalene went alone on Easter morning to look for the grave of Jesus. When she was still some distance away she could see that the stone that was used to close the entrance of the burial chamber had been rolled away. Without even going to take a look into the empty chamber, she hurried off to Peter and to the "disciple whom Jesus loved" to tell them: "The Lord has been taken out of the grave and we do not know where they have laid him." The use of the word "we" could be a trace of the tradition-form that the Synoptics used, where Magdalene is said to have gone with other women to the grave.

Peter and the other disciple (who was not one of the twelve, but was one of the closer followers of Jesus) now hurried to the burial place. Luke also (24:12) tells us of Peter going to the grave (without companions). This old tradition-report was taken up by the fourth evangelist, but he adds mention of a companion with Peter. The detail that follows is found only in John's report: the other disciple ran faster than Peter. He came first to the grave and saw the linen wrappings lying there, but he did not go in. Peter arrived later and went into the chamber and verified that the linen wrappings were there, and also that the handkerchief that had been placed over the head of Jesus had been put in a special place. Then the other disciple also went in; he saw and he believed (20:8). This almost pedantically-stated description is given to rule out the idea that there was a grave robbery: such thieves would have taken away the body with all its wrappings. There is a further meaning in the passage: it shows the higher position given to Peter, as well as the authority of the other disciple, who enjoyed a very high repute among the groups in which the Fourth Gospel was written. It may be that the two disciples symbolize the two branches of Christianity, Jewish and Gentile, and their relation to the resurrection-faith: the Jews arrived first and after them the Gentiles, but the readiness to believe was greater in the Gentile Christians than among the Jews.

If after this we read (v 9) of both disciples: "They did not yet know from the Scriptures that he had to rise from the dead," the accent must most likely be put on the "had to" statement. They recorded the fact of the empty grave, but they did not yet understand that the death and resurrection of Jesus were in accordance with the Scriptures and corresponded to the revealed will of God as given in the Old Testament.

THE APPARITIONS OF THE RISEN ONE

Excepting only Mark, all the other evangelists record that the risen Jesus was seen several times by his followers. It is difficult, if not impossible, to bring the different reports into agreement. The fact still stands, and is also witnessed by 1 Corinthians 15:5–7, that Jesus revealed himself to his own as one who had risen from the dead.

In reading the Easter accounts of the Gospels we must always keep in mind that they have not been written with the intention of being historical reports as we think of them today. Their main concern is giving witness for the resurrection. They do contain historical recollections which are often much reworked. Especially the fourth evangelist made changes to put them in the form of theological reports. In what follows only two of these reports will be discussed.

The Apparition Seen by Mary Magdalene
(Jn 20:11–18)

While the early evangelists tell us that the angel of revelation announced the Easter message to the women who came to the grave, in the Fourth Gospel this announcement is made by Jesus himself. Only he is the valid witness for the resurrection-faith of the Church.

Apparently Mary Magdalene, who brought the news of the empty grave to the apostles, came back to the grave and lamented that the body of Jesus was gone. There she saw two angels sitting in the burial chamber, and they asked her why she was weeping. Mary answered, mentioning Jesus' name, and then turned, before they could tell her the Easter news. She saw Jesus standing there without recognizing that it was Jesus. She supposed it to be the gardener (the incident took place in a garden). Since she supposed that the gardener could have taken the body away, she said to him: "Sir, if you have carried him off, tell me where you have put him, and I will take him away." Her desire to have the body of Jesus is mostly a natural human one, understandable as an expression of her great love of Jesus. The evangelist seems to hear in this entreaty some longing for an enduring communion with the Lord.

Then Jesus lets her know who he is by simply speaking her name. That one word was enough to startle her intensely and she could only answer with the word "Rabboni" (my Lord, my Master), a title of majesty which the Jews used in addressing Yahweh; it is used in only one other place in the New Testament, in Mark 10:51, as referring to

Jesus. In reply Jesus said: "Do not cling to me, for I have not yet gone up to my Father."

Apparently, in her spontaneous expression of joy at seeing him again, she had grasped his feet; we read in Matthew 28:9 that the women did this too when Jesus appeared to them. But it is puzzling why Jesus should have added the command that she should not cling to him any longer. And we might ask also what he means when he speaks of going up to the Father. It could hardly be the ascension that Luke speaks of in 24:51; rather it is the exaltation and the glorification that came already with the death on the cross, but was not yet completely realized. In particular, his followers had not yet been given any share in this. But since Jesus had elsewhere explained to his disciples (Jn 14:3) his return to the Father as something yet to come, he can say here that he has not yet gone ahead to him. The message that Mary should take to the disciples is this: "I am going up to him who is my Father and your Father, to my God and to your God." This is the paraphrase of the evangelist John for the ancient Christian Easter message: He has been raised. In the waking up of his only Son the Father has shown Jesus as his God and has not failed the trust of his Son. Hence the disciples also can trust in him without reserve.

In going now to the disciples and announcing to them, "I have seen the Lord," she does not mean that she has had a simple look at him; hers is rather a faithful view in which Jesus the Lord, the Son of God, is recognized. And where the evangelist lets Mary say to the disciples, "I have seen the Lord," he probably wants to bring out the fact that the witness of his resurrection who was delegated to bring the Easter message was a woman, something unheard of in Jewish practice.

The Appearance to the Eleven Disciples
(Mt 28:16–20)

In his Gospel Matthew tells us only of two apparitions of the risen One: the first one to Mary Magdalene and another Mary on Easter morning (28:9f), and the second one that makes up the conclusion of his Gospel and is a summary of the whole good news that Matthew reports. These five concluding verses are, from a verbal point of view, a masterpiece of expression; it would be impossible to say more and greater things in fifty words.

The evangelist first tells us that the eleven disciples, who still made up the circle of closest disciples after the departure of the traitor Judas, were back in Galilee "on the mountain that Jesus had told them about." This is a reference to a theological expression rather than a geographical one; it concerns the place of the Sermon on the Mount (cf. Mt 5:1), where Jesus had begun his public ministry. There also should be the place where it would conclude. Hence the evangelist is saying that the risen One who revealed himself on the mountain is none other than that Jesus of Nazareth, who had brought the revelation of God to mankind during his earthly life. His final word of revelation is a proclamation of the Church that would come to be.

The text does not say explicitly that Jesus appeared to the disciples. But from the remark that "as they saw Jesus, they fell down before him" this is self-evident. This prostration in worship gives evidence of their readiness to acknowledge the divine dignity of Jesus. But the evangelist adds that "they were still doubtful." (This is the literal translation rather than the one more commonly found: *some* had doubts.) The sentence proves that in the very early Church the faith in the resurrection was not taken as self-evident. The doubt of the disciples in the resurrection of Jesus is evident in all the reports that the Gospels give of the apparitions. Hence the risen One always refers in his meetings with the disciples to the fact that he is the one who had been crucified. The objection that the credulous disciples were guilty of self-deception was countered by the evangelists in the way by which they told how difficult it was for Jesus to overcome their doubts and their lack of faith.

To remove such doubts Matthew has Jesus speak the powerful words that convey the meaning of the Easter event in the most concise way: "All authority in heaven and on earth has been given to me." Such a colossal assertion by a human being means: God has raised up the crucified one and established him as the bearer of the final revelation, and as the one who proclaims the eternal divine majesty. He has been given an exclusive, unique, irreplaceable position in the history of salvation. What is still to come in the establishment of the kingdom of God is now bound up with the person of Jesus. Through him God will reveal his power and render salvation to the earth. The power of the risen One encompasses everything that is involved in the divine plan of salvation. What Jesus says of himself here is taken up by Mark 16:19 and given in the profession of faith: he was "taken up to heaven and is seated now at the right hand of God."

To this statement of omnipotence Matthew adds the final commission: "Therefore you must go and make disciples of all nations." Nowhere else in the Gospels do we find such a universal missionary commitment expressed. In saying this, the evangelist wishes to make evident the importance of the Easter event for the Church and for all of mankind. As the Acts of the Apostles shows, once the proclamation of the Gospel went beyond the borders of Israel it was taken up by more and more people in the Mediterranean basin.

The continuation of the missionary command tells the disciples how they should proceed in their mission work: "Baptize them in the name of the Father and the Son and the Holy Spirit, and teach them to observe all the commandments which I have given you." Only Matthew speaks of a baptism in the name of the three divine Persons. The form given by Paul, "to baptize in Christ Jesus" (Rom 6:3) and the common form given in Acts (8:16; 19:5), "in the name of the Lord Jesus," are certainly older. They stress the essential effect of baptism; through this sacrament the one baptized becomes Jesus' own. There can hardly be question that it was in this earlier form that baptism was administered.

The extension of the baptismal formula to include the three persons of the Trinity was made during the second Christian generation. It did not change or falsify the meaning of baptism; it simply took over an expression of apostolic tradition. Indeed one could not rightly preach of Christ as the bringer of salvation without also mentioning God the Father who had sent his Son as our Savior. Paul often speaks of God, Christ, and the Spirit working together (cf. 1 Cor 12:4–6; 2 Cor 13:13). Matthew's baptismal formula expresses in concise form the cooperation and the unity of Father, Son, and Spirit. In the biblical view the name of a person indicates its nature and its purpose. The fact that we have "in the name" given only once, thereby taking the three persons together, causes the formula to indicate that the unity of the effect is based on the unity of the being.

Most likely this formula is not original with Matthew; he adopted the baptismal formula that had already become

common in his time. In giving it as something spoken by
Jesus himself he is only following the practice of the evangelists in attributing to Jesus words that were first formulated in the early Church. The important point is that the
Trinitarian baptismal formula is in accord with revelation.
In it, what the apostolic preaching taught about the cooperation of the Father, Christ, and the Spirit found its prac-
tical expression.

The mission command of Jesus also says: "Teach them
to observe all the commandments which I have given you."
The terms "teach" and "command" are characteristic of
Matthew. "All that I have commanded you" means the will
of God, as shown by Jesus in his lifetime and as put by him
in the commandment of love. Through his resurrection
from the dead his teaching received its final approbation;
it is the seal of approval for the whole plan of life for the
people of God.

The Christ raised up to God is the Teacher absolutely.
A teaching of his disciples can happen only by mandate of
Jesus. This means taking on a task of great responsibility.
The disciples should teach only what Jesus has told them
to, and must proclaim it unshortened. And it is not enough
for them just to make statements about the message of Jesus; they must also live it for mankind to see.

The conclusion of Jesus' discourse to the eleven disciples is a promise of help for them: "Be sure of this: I am
with you all days until the end of the world." In these words
again we recognize the divine power of the risen One. The
formula "I am with thee" or "with you" is found frequently
in the Old Testament when Yahweh gives mandates to the
leaders of Israel or when he addresses the whole people,
especially when he asks something difficult of them. In the
first chapter of his Gospel, Matthew tells Mary that the
Messiah-child she was to bear should be given the name

Immanuel, that is, "God-with-us" (1:23). At the end of his writing he now shows that through Easter this promise has been fulfilled. Jesus, the risen One, is for us now the present divine Lord, always near at hand. His word concerns not only the eleven; it is directed to all to whom they should proclaim the message of salvation and the discipleship that would come after that first Easter. It is Jesus who is God present among mankind for all his people since his resurrection.

Neither the two reports of appearances that have been discussed here, nor the others that are found in the Gospels, try to explain how we should conceive them. They simply stress the identity of the risen One with Jesus of Nazareth, and the fact that he appeared in a real body. Luke 24:36ff tells us that Jesus showed the disciples his hands and feet, and even told them to touch him. He has them give him a piece of roasted fish, and he eats it in front of them. John 20:27 has Jesus tell the unbelieving Thomas to put a hand in his side. Thomas is granted this "sign" of touching the body of Christ because he belonged to the first generation, through whose word all later generations should come to the faith. These later generations could base their faith only on the witness of those first disciples. This is the meaning of the appearances of the risen One. He wanted to give unmistakable testimony to his disciples of the reality of his triumph over death. Today we Christians can agree without question to the fifth article of the symbol and thereby show that we belong to those for whom the Beatitude of Jesus counts: "Blessed are those who do not see but believe just the same" (Jn 20:29).

VI
HE ASCENDED INTO HEAVEN AND IS SEATED AT THE RIGHT HAND OF GOD THE ALMIGHTY FATHER

The profession of faith in the ascension of Jesus into heaven is a source of considerable difficulty for many Christians in these times. For the idea of "ascension into heaven" presumes a picture of the world that no longer corresponds with that of our times. In the age of spaceship travel it seems naive to speak of a flat earth over which there is a cover of heavenly clouds in which God is enthroned. And when there is a statement in the symbol that "he sits at the right hand of the Father" this is also an impossible presentation. As a pure spirit God does not have a body and cannot have a left or right hand. But if we look for the pertinent texts in the Bible and study their meaning, these difficulties are easily removed.

The idea of ascension into heaven, or, better expressed, an "elevation" of Jesus, is found already in the earliest of the New Testament writings. Paul mentions it in his First Epistle to the Thessalonians between the year 50 and 52, where he says they expect the Son of God to come from heaven: "Jesus, whom he raised from the dead" (1 Thess 1:10). While an elevation to God is not explicitly mentioned, it is presumed. Apparently Paul considered the resurrection of Jesus as also including his elevation to God at the same time. In the Epistle to the Romans (written between 55 and 57) the same apostle says: "Christ Jesus, who died for us, and who has risen again and sits at the right hand of God, is pleading for us" (8:34). Here also the ascension into heaven is not explicitly mentioned, but the seat at the right of God is implied in what has been said about the resurrection from the dead.

At the end of the sixteenth chapter of the oldest Gospel the ascension of Jesus is mentioned: "When he had finished speaking to them the Lord Jesus was taken up to heaven, and is seated now at the right hand of God" (Mk 16:19). This ending of the sixteenth chapter is, however, not a part of the original Gospel; it was added only in the second century. Verse 19 is an abbreviated synopsis of Luke 24:50–53 and Acts 1:9–11. Nevertheless, it is noteworthy that the two expressions "taken up to heaven" and "seated at the right hand of God" were already in the text of the Apostles' Creed in the second century.

Matthew also tells us nothing of the ascension of Jesus. The last words of his Gospel are: "I am with you through all the days that are coming until the end of the world" (28:20), and they seem to exclude such an idea of an ascension. But there is an indirect reference of an exaltation of Jesus, since his statement "All authority in heaven and earth has been given to me" (28:18) presumes such higher dignity: he speaks as one on whom God has already bestowed dominion over all creation.

Luke is the first to speak, in both his writings, the Gospel and Acts of the Apostles (written between years 90 and 95), of an ascension of Jesus into heaven. In the Gospel (24:36–43) he tells of an appearance of the risen Jesus to the eleven disciples on the evening of Easter Day in Jerusalem. In the course of this meeting Jesus tried to convince his faithful ones of the reality of his resurrection and gave them the command to remain in the city until they were "clothed with power from on high" by the Holy Spirit.

"Then he took them out as far as Bethany. There he lifted up his hands and blessed them. And even as he blessed them he parted from them and was carried up to heaven" (24:50f). According to this text therefore the ascension took place in the evening of the day of the resurrection.

In the version given in Acts, Luke adds to what he wrote in the Gospel, but he prefaces his statements with the remark that "he had shown them (the apostles) by many proofs that he was still alive after his passion; throughout the course of forty days he had been appearing to them and telling them about the kingdom of God" (1:3). Jesus gives them the instruction that they should wait in Jerusalem for the "fulfillment of the Father's promise" and then to go out to the whole world as his witnesses. "When he had said this they saw him lifted up, and a cloud caught him away from their sight" (v 9).

This is the first place where the ascension date is fixed as the fortieth day after Easter. Luke is quietly correcting his earlier notice at the end of his Gospel, which said that we must take the day of the ascension to be the same as that of Easter. He now knows of later appearances of the risen One and must tell of them, thus being required to write in order to make the apostles reliable witnesses of the Savior's resurrection.

The evangelist uses a description already available in the Old Testament in order to depict the final carrying away of Jesus from his own followers. In Genesis 5:24 we read of Enoch: "Enoch walked with God. Then he vanished because God had taken him." The taking up of the prophet Elijah is described with particular detail in 2 Kings 2. While he was talking to his disciple Elisha, a fiery chariot appeared, pulled by fiery horses, and separated the two men. In the sight of Elisha, Elijah was taken up to heaven in a whirlwind (2:11f). The expression "he was taken up to heaven" (Lk 24:51) is in literal agreement with 1 Maccabees 2:58, as also with the description of Elijah.

The verses of Acts 1:9–11 indicate extensive formulation by Luke; it is questionable whether he could rely altogether on older traditions, and instead wrote these verses himself. The expression "he was taken up in their sight" corresponds to the other one: "A cloud took him up and drew him away from their view." Both stress the eye-witness evidence of the apostles. For Luke only those who had been present from the baptism of Jesus to his ascension could be considered as witnesses of the resurrection of Jesus (cf. Acts 1:21f). Hence the ascension is also the last appearance of Jesus; in it he made his final departure from the sight of his disciples. The evangelist is not concerned with portrayal of past events; his main interest is in establishing that this was the last meeting of Jesus with the apostles.

Most likely Luke does not consider the clouds that took Jesus from their view as an actual vapor-cover that came over the sky. In the old covenant clouds are symbols for the presence of God; they indicate his presence and also conceal his glory. At the consecration of Solomon's temple a cloud filled the house of the Lord and the priests could not carry out their duties (2 Chr 5:14). The clouds that appeared at the transfiguration of Jesus and cast their shadow on the three disciples are a symbol of the divine presence; from that cloud came the voice of God the Father: "This is my beloved Son; you should listen to him" (Lk 9:34f). Hence we can say that in the account of the ascension the clouds indicate only the meaning of this incident: the taking up of Jesus into full community with God is an inexpressible mystery.

Finally we can also say that the appearance of two angels is a means used by the evangelists to emphasize an important truth: this Jesus, whom the disciples saw taken up to heaven, will come again. The readers of the Acts of the Apostles should, along with the disciples, attain the certainty that this event will come to pass sometime, but it is not in the near future. The departure of Jesus has opened, according to Luke, a new epoch in the history of salvation: the time of the Church.

In three places John's Gospel makes brief mention of the ascension of Jesus. In the third chapter the evangelist inserts into the talk of Jesus with Nicodemus a section composed by himself (vv 13–21, 31–36). The introductory sentence says: "No man has ever gone up to heaven except the one who has come down from heaven, the Son of Man." Here the author takes a position against those in the world around him who entertain fantasies about heavenly journeys in ecstasy or about rising above the world of matter into the kingdom of light. John vigorously rejects such chimeras. He considers only one exception: only the Son of Man (a name of honor for Jesus) has gone up to heaven. He can do this because he had come down from heaven in the incarnation. What was sung in the ancient Christian hymn of the Epistle to the Philippians (2:7–9) is expressed here also: the self-abnegation of the Son of God corresponds to his exaltation.

John introduces the account of the Last Supper of Jesus with his disciples in these words: "Jesus knew that the hour had come for his passage from this world to the Father" (13:1). Here "passage" means the same as "being taken up" or "ascension" in the words of the other evangelists; the only difference is that the point of arrival is given as God, the Father of Jesus, rather than heaven.

We have already seen another reference to the ascension into heaven in a different context. In the rather obscure dialogue of the risen One with Mary Magdalene we read: "Do not cling to me for I have not yet gone up to my Father" (20:17). The expression "to go up" brings up the image of a passage to heaven, but here John is most likely speaking of the exaltation of Jesus, which he speaks of also in other places. In this way he is describing both the exaltation on the cross and the glorification of Jesus. He sees death, resurrection, and glorification as a unity.

As the risen One Jesus is already on high (cf. in the same verse 17: "I am going up to my God and your God, to my Father and your Father"). But he still has one task to fulfill for his disciples: he must impart to them full community with the Father, and this includes also the sending of the Holy Spirit (according to John 20:22 this took place in the evening of the same day). The difference between "I have not yet ascended" and "I am going up" should not be understood as a sequence in time. It is a paraphrase for the theological statement that, as one risen and glorified, Jesus must complete his work through his disciples who have not yet gone with him into final glory.

In summary one can say: Faith in the exaltation of the human nature of Jesus is a part of the original deposit of faith. It follows from the resurrection from the dead. Since then Jesus is the exalted One, living with the Father. Where Luke has put an interval of forty days between Easter and the ascension, he does this to gain time in his narrative for the appearances of Jesus to his disciples. Sitting at the right hand of the Father is naturally only a metaphor; to let Jesus sit at his right hand means to give him highest honor. To have Jesus sit at the right hand of the Father expresses his natural equality with God and the highest glorification of his human nature. Being taken up does not mean that the omnipresent God has been put in some definite place in heaven. John speaks of a passing over to the Father, which indicates the meaning somewhat better than to speak of an ascension into heaven; it says that Jesus has gone on to the other world of God which surpasses our understanding.

VII
FROM WHENCE HE WILL COME TO JUDGE
THE LIVING AND THE DEAD

This following article about his return to judge the living and the dead is closely connected with the article of faith concerning the ascension. Luke already ties the two together when he has two men come up after the account of the ascension who tell the disciples: "You men of Galilee, why are you standing there and looking up to heaven? This Jesus who has left you and been taken up to heaven is the same one who will come back again in the same way that you have seen him go from here" (Acts 1:11).

In Greek texts this return is designated by the word "parousia." Originally this word meant presence or actuality, but it was also used to denote an arrival by which someone became present. In non-biblical use of the word, "parousia" often describes the advent of a divine being who gives witness of his presence by some powerful act. It is also used to describe the visit of the emperor or some other high official going to a province. In writings of Christian authors the word almost always means the coming of the glorified Christ to bring judgment at the end of the world. Ignatius of Antioch (about the year 110) describes the coming of God in the incarnation as "parousia." Hence we hear of a first and a second parousia; there is also mention of the second one as "the return."

Jesus often speaks in the Gospels of the coming of the Son of Man in judgment. Thus we read in Mark 8:38: "If

anyone is ashamed of acknowledging me and my words before this unfaithful and wicked generation, the Son of Man,
when he comes in his Father's glory with the holy angels, will
be ashamed to acknowledge him." From the context we see
that here "to be ashamed" means to be unwilling to follow
Jesus in the way of the cross. In the judgment the Lord will
consider such a person as one who does not belong to him.

Mark tells us of the hearing given to Jesus by the high
council during the narrative of the passion. It does not
bring to light why a condemnation to death should be
granted. Finally the high priest asks him: "Are you the
Messiah, the Son of the One most highly praised?" Jesus
answered: "I am. And you will see the Son of Man sitting
at the right hand of God's power, and coming with the
clouds of heaven" (14:61f). These words are not an early
Christian profession that was later given as something spoken by Jesus. They prove themselves to be truly Jesus'
words. According to Jewish customs of those times it was
forbidden to use God's name; the metaphor of "the Power"
was used to replace it. Sitting at the right hand is a reference to Psalm 110:1, and the coming of the Son of Man in
the clouds is a reference to Daniel 7:13. There can be no
doubt here that Jesus considers himself to be the Son of
Man, and his coming in judgment is predicted.

Luke also speaks of the coming of the Son of Man in
17:22–37. Here the evangelist has brought together a se-
ries of texts, all of them dealing with the parousia and the
sudden appearance of Christ in final judgment; no one can
escape it, and no one can predict it from signs and omens.
"The Son of Man, when his time comes, will be like the
lightning which lightens from one border of heaven to the
other" (17:24). Here the Son of Man means Jesus, and his
day means the parousia. Many interpreters maintain er-
roneously that the title Son of Man was first applied to Je-

sus by the early Church, and that he himself meant someone else. The expression is found only in the Gospels; it is not found in Paul's writings or in early Christian professions of faith. Hence we accept that Jesus names himself in this way to avoid the misunderstood title of Messiah. Later Christians had no reason to shrink from considering Jesus to be both Messiah and Son of God. Hence the expression "Son of Man" dropped out of the vernacular.

The parousia is often called "that day" in John's Gospel. The expression comes from the Old Testament and refers to the day of Yahweh at the end of time, which means a day both of salvation and of judgment. In his farewell talk (Jn 13–16), Jesus tells his disciples of his return, but rather soon, and not on some far-distant day (14:3, 18, 28). The reference here is, then, most likely to his coming in the resurrection; after that his return is continual in the experience of the Spirit (14:16–18). In this way the day of Yahweh refers also to the present.

Most of all, the letters of Paul indicate how lively was the faith in the parousia among those of the early Church—for instance in 1 Thessalonians 4:13—5:11, where it is depicted as apocalyptic revelation in glory. The word "maranatha" used in the liturgy (cf. 1 Cor 16:22), also taken over literally in its Aramaic form by the communities of the diaspora, expresses the longing for imminent coming of the parousia; it means "(our) Lord comes" or rather: "Come, Lord."

THE ESCHATOLOGICAL DISCOURSE
(MARK 13)

There is detailed treatment of the return of Christ in what has been called the "eschatological discourse" (all of Chapter 13 in Mark). Jesus delivered it in the Garden of

Olives shortly before his passion, we read in verse 3. But it is almost certain that the text, as we read it in Mark, was not delivered in this fashion by Jesus. In its interpretation the discourse is still very much disputed. The explanation given by F. Hahn and modified by R. Pesch has probably found the most agreement. According to it, a Jewish-Christian wrote it about the time of the beginning of the Jewish war (66–70 A.D.) as an instructional teaching. The author had as sources both the words of Jesus and the explanation of the prophecy of Daniel, and he placed the statements in contemporary context.

This discourse was in circulation in the original community and caused anxiety and fear among the faithful. When the evangelist Mark took it to hand he decided to put it into his already completed Gospel, making certain necessary corrections and avoiding wrong interpretations. What Daniel 9:27 calls the "abominable desolation" the author refers to the destruction of the temple in Jerusalem, spoken of also in an old prophetic statement of Jesus. This he put at the beginning of the discourse (v 2) in order to emphasize the expectation of the end of the world by the account of the destruction of the temple (v 33). He says that the mission to the Gentiles must come before the end and he warns explicitly against fanatical preachers of the parousia (v 10 and v 6).

In the first part of Mark 13 the discourse is about the hardships and the temptations that would come in the last days. The author of these descriptions, writing before the time of Mark, speaks of the wars and persecutions and the appearance of false messiahs, using Old Testament texts and apocalyptic imagery then in widespread circulation.

The high point of the discourse on the last times, in which the parousia and its place in time are discussed, is in verses 24–27. "In those days, after great distress, the sun will be darkened and the moon's light will disappear; the stars will fall from heaven, and the powers in the heavens will be shaken" (vv 24f). The double time-designations, "in those days" and "after the great distress," separate what follows from the afflictions (wars, persecutions, the rise of false messiahs) mentioned before. Hence this is no longer enumeration of things that are in the nature of grim catastrophes: dimming of sources of light and shaking of heavenly powers is only saying that the end of present world time is immediately ahead.

The evangelist depicts the essential event in only one sentence: "Then they will see the Son of Man coming upon the clouds with great power and glory" (v 26). The judgment of the world and the conquest of satanic powers is not mentioned. He tells only of the coming of the Son of Man, in terms borrowed from Daniel 7:13: "One like the son of man came on the clouds of heaven . . . to him will be given sovereignty and honor and kingship." There is disagreement whether the prophet Daniel takes the son of man here as a symbol for the people of Israel or for a single sovereign person. But in any case Mark identifies him with Jesus. He should be recognized by the clouds on which he comes as a divine person.

The purpose of his coming is not mentioned; what is important is that the undetermined ones, who should recognize his coming, include, first of all, the enemies of the Messiah, for whom he comes in judgment. In spite of the apocalyptic images that are not to be taken literally, the event described—that Jesus, the risen Lord taken up to God, will return again—must be firmly held.

The assembling of the chosen ones, the faithful, is given in verse 27 as the last act in the events of those last days. The angels take part in this: they appear elsewhere as the harvest workers of the judgment; for example we read in Matthew 13:39: "The end of the world is the harvest; it is reaped by the angels." That is the way the evangelist Matthew interprets the parable of the weeds. Where we hear of the chosen ones "from all points of the compass" being brought together, it means that all faithful, wherever they are at the time of the parousia, will be assembled and brought to Jesus. The expression "from the ends of the earth to the ends of the heavens" serves also to indicate the all-encompassing extent of the final event.

The discourse on the end of time that we find in Mark does not mention the resurrection of the dead nor the judgment of the enemies of Christ. It speaks only of the assembling of the elect who are still alive at the time of the parousia. By his very brief description of the event the evangelist indicates that the coming world is indescribable and is beyond human curiosity.

THE QUESTION ABOUT THE FINAL END

At the beginning of the discourse (Mk 13:4) the disciples ask Jesus: "Tell us when this will be, and what sign will be given, when all this will be about to be fulfilled?" Verses 28–32 try to give the answer to these questions. Obviously anyone who expects to hear of an exact terminal date will be disappointed. The veil that covers the mystery may, at most, be slightly lifted; it will never be removed.

An absolutely certain, but not calculable, connection between the announcement of the end and its arrival is suggested by the image of the fig tree (v 28). In contrast to the many evergreen trees of Palestine, the fig tree sheds its leaves in the autumn and produces new ones in the spring; hence it indicates the beginning of a new season of the year. In winter its branches seem to be completely dead. But when the sap rises anew in them they become flexible and bring out new leaves. In this way they show that summer is at hand.

The application of the metaphor is in verse 29. In the original text this reads: "So you, when you see all this come about, are to know that it is near, at your door." It does not say who or what is near. One can add: the end, or the Son of Man, or, comprehensively: judgment and salvation. The events of the last days indicate the nearness of the divine majesty; in the coming of the Son of Man this divine consummation is completed.

There is a solemn formula of introduction, "Amen I say to you," to certify the prophetic text: "This generation will not have passed away before all this is accomplished" (v 30). Here "this generation" means all those living at the time of Jesus. In the Gospels the expression has a somewhat negative association; for instance Mark 8:38 says: "this unfaithful and wicked generation." The evangelist, who had found this prophecy in tradition, does not deny the possibility of imminence of the parousia and the end of the world. For him, however, faithfulness of the Christian to the end is more important than calculation of the time of the parousia. Hence the following verse 31 emphasizes the permanence of the word of Jesus. Heaven and earth, that is, all creation, has an end at some time; but the word of Jesus, that is, his whole proclamation, will not pass away in eternity. In this the evangelist Mark is telling his readers that even if the parousia is not immediately at hand, the teaching of Jesus will not pass away.

Verse 32 is a difficult one to explain: "But as for that day and that hour, nobody knows it: not even the angels in heaven or the Son, but only the Father." It is hard to see how this could have come from Jesus himself; it is something that was added by the evangelist. In opposition to the apocalyptics who gave the impression that they knew the exact hour when the Lord would return, Mark stresses the fact that God alone arranges the schedule of final events, and hence he has reserved to himself the knowledge of the time of its coming. "That day" is the day of judgment; "that hour" means a still closer fixing. The threefold negation (nobody—not the angels—not even the Son) aims at stopping all wild imagination about the day of the parousia. Only God knows it. Human beings cannot look at his cards. God alone is the Lord of history and only he can determine its final phase.

Thus we have the answer of the evangelists to the question of the "when" of the end of the world (v 4). For the present we have only hints and forebodings about the nearness of the end. The Jewish war and the destruction of the temple particularly gave a first foretaste of the last miseries. Whoever believes, however, and trusts in the word of Jesus need not fear about the end.

THE IMMINENCE OF THE PAROUSIA

If after all that has been said, even by Jesus, about the lack of knowledge of the time of the end of the world, how is it that many of the things he says seem to assume that the final events are close at hand? For instance, according to Mark 9:1 (8:39 in some versions) he said: "Amen I say to you: There are those standing here who will not taste of death before they have seen the Son of Man coming in his kingdom." Here we have an old saying that the evangelist found in traditional sources he was using, but it can hardly be a genuine word of Jesus. In any case, Mark takes it as a point of decision or of "no return" that can be understood as a statement of the final return, since it brings the parousia in association with the transfiguration of Jesus. For he tells of this with the words of introduction "six days afterward." His meaning is: for some of those present, namely for the apostles Peter, James, and John, the promise has been fulfilled in their being witnesses of his transfiguration. In a certain sense this was an anticipated parousia.

It is clear from all that the Gospels say about Jesus' preaching of the final times that he was convinced of the coming exaltation of God. By his works this advent of divinity came into this world; in its complete majesty however it is still to come. It seems that toward the end of his life he predicted the destruction of Jerusalem, but he did not put it as coincidental with the parousia. In expressions of imminence he speaks of his own future. As for the future of mankind he knows that it will carry on after his death. But he does not give any fixed determination; he calls to all to be watchful and to be prepared for the hour when the parousia will come.

The evangelist Luke takes a particular position about the imminence of the parousia. He does not reject the traditional eschatology; he believes in the return of Christ at the end of the world. But he does not count on the immediate carrying out of this event. He is more interested in the fate of individual souls after death. For everyone the future of the world becomes present at the instant of death. He illustrates this in the parable of the rich landowner (Lk 12:16–21), found only in his Gospel. The landowner thought only of the immediate interests of his wealth; what use it had for his fortune in the future beyond he did not consider. The evangelist sums up in this way: "Thus it is for those who lay up treasure for themselves and have no credit with God."

Another text found only in Luke corresponds to this:

"Make use of your base wealth to win friends for yourself so that, when you leave that wealth behind, they will welcome you into eternal homes" (16:9). The point in time when the decision comes is not the last day; rather, it is the day of death for each soul. Everything depends on having eternal treasure in heaven at that instant (cf. 12:33). These and similar texts show that Luke discounts the events of the end of the world in order to emphasize the meaning of the death of the individual person.

THE FINAL JUDGMENT

Faith in the judgment pronounced on the living and the dead is associated with the parousia. Discourses and sayings recorded in the Gospels of Jesus refer often to the judgment of reward and punishment. Thus we hear of a warning spoken by Jesus that at the day of judgment the men of Nineveh will rise up with this generation and will condemn it (Mt 12:41). In the parable of the weeds among the grain (Mt 13:24–30) the talk is about harvest time for a field in which both wheat and weeds are growing. Only then will the harvesters separate the weeds from the grain. They bind the weeds in bundles to be burned; the wheat they bring to the barn.

Already in the prophets of the Old Testament we read of the harvest as a figure for the judgment. Only at the final judgment will there be separation of the good from the wicked; only then will come the decision about participation in divine glory. The interpretation of the parable that is given (Mt 13:36–43) does not come from Jesus himself. In it the harvest is explicitly compared with the end of the world, and the angels are likened to the harvesters whom the Son of Man will send out to gather up all violators of the law in his kingdom and will throw them into the fiery furnace: "There will be weeping and gnashing of teeth." Often in the Gospels the punishment of hellfire is expressed in these words. The lot of the good people is described in a single sentence in this context. "Then the just will shine out like the sun in the kingdom of their Father." That the Son of Man is the judge is indicated by the fact that he sends out the angels.

The author of Matthew's Gospel has put three pieces together in chapter 25, all of them dealing with the final judgment: the parable of the ten bridesmaids (vv 1–13), the parables of the money held in trust (vv 14–30), and finally the extended description of the judgment of the world (vv 31–46). In the last-mentioned piece the Son of Man is represented explicitly as the judge now come into his glory as the risen Christ. For Judaism God himself is the judge; here the evangelist transfers this supreme function to Christ. The judgment befalls all people, Jews and Gentiles, and it presumes the general resurrection of all the dead. The activity of the judge is presented as the task of a shepherd separating the sheep from the goats in his flock in the evening. As they are made to take their places to the right and to the left of the judge these sides become the symbols of the separation of the saved from the damned. The virtuous ones are invited to take their places in the kingdom prepared for them from the beginning of the world because they helped the king in many of his needs. Those so favored expressed great astonishment over the basis for this judgment. After all, they had never seen Jesus in any great need and could not have helped him. But he gave them the answer: "What you did for the least of my brethren you did for me." "Brethren" here does not mean just the disciples of Jesus then present; it means all mankind reduced to misery and need. Jesus identifies himself with the needy of all nations and all times. All love shown for fellow men and women is also love of Jesus and of God.

The judge pronounces corresponding sentences on those standing to his left: "Go away from me, you that are accursed, into the eternal fire that has been prepared for the devil and his angels." The basis for this sentence is the same, and the sentence is carried out: "These shall pass on to eternal punishment, and the just shall go on to eternal life."

This depiction of the last judgment should not be understood as a prophetic description of its procedure. There are similar accounts of the judgment in the Jewish literature of those times. It is hardly likely that Jesus ever spoke a discourse of this kind; it is difficult to imagine that he would condemn souls to eternal punishment in such harsh words. The very titles of honor that the text gives to Jesus—Shepherd, King, Lord, Son of the Father—were not ones that we would expect the earthly Jesus to give to himself; they come from the profession of faith of the early Church. Hence one believes that an apocalyptic Jewish description of what God or his Messiah said was taken over and attributed to Jesus. But its use in the Gospel shows clearly that the ancient Church actually held that Jesus is the coming judge and that his judgment was connected with the parousia.

The return of Christ in judgment is still a firm article of Christian faith; however, revelation does not tell us anything definite about the time when it will come or the details of its procedure; apocalyptic descriptions of the scene cannot count as statements of faith.

VIII
I BELIEVE IN THE HOLY SPIRIT

The first article of the Creed states belief in God the Father, and the six articles following are professions concerning Christ. The eighth article is dedicated to the third person of the Trinity, the Holy Spirit. It concludes the profession of faith in the mystery of the Trinity. This mystery of faith has its biblical foundation in the commission that the risen Jesus gave his disciples: to go to all nations, making disciples of them and baptizing them "in the name of the Father and of the Son and of the Holy Spirit" (Mt 28:19).

This form-statement of baptism that paraphrases the profession of faith in the Trinity can scarcely have come from Jesus himself. From earlier writings of the New Testament we learn that baptism was originally conferred "in the name of Jesus." This would be inconceivable if Jesus himself had revealed the Trinitarian baptismal formula. Hence we must conclude that Matthew put into his writing, as words coming from Jesus himself, the baptismal formula being used in the community for whom he wrote the Gospel.

Baptism in the name of Jesus says that Christ is the bringer of salvation and the one being baptized is devoted to him. But Jesus can only be the bearer of salvation if God the Father has sent him for this purpose. According to Paul there is no Christian existence without the Spirit of God through whom the exalted Christ carried out his work.

Thus the salvation that is brought to the Christian in baptism is the gift of Father, Son, and Spirit all at once. The influence of the earthly Jesus seen in his reference to the Trinity can be found early in Christian writings, as, for example, in Acts 10:38, where Peter says in one of his discourses: "You have heard . . . how God anointed Jesus of Nazareth with the Holy Spirit and with power, so that he went about doing good and curing all . . . for God was with him."

The eighth article of the apostolic symbol is a profession of the divinity of the Spirit, even if it does not explicitly say so. Only in the Council of Constantinople in 381 was it found necessary to condemn false teaching by stating the doctrine more explicitly; hence it stated that he is the "Lord" and the "giver of life" who proceeds from the Father and the Son and is worshiped together with them. What had been implicitly believed earlier was thus expressly professed.

Very often in the Gospels the Spirit of God is mentioned but the places where he is clearly seen as a person are not very many. Often "Spirit" means the same as the "force" or the "power" of God, as for instance when the angel spoke to Mary at the annunciation: "The Holy Spirit will come upon you and the power of the most high will overshadow you" (Lk 1:35). The two phrases have the same meaning; they state one idea: only divine Omnipotence can effect the incarnation of the Son of God.

The Gospel accounts of the baptism of Jesus in the Jordan tell us of the bestowal of the Holy Spirit on him (Mk 1:10 and parallels). From that moment he was under the guidance of the spirit. The spirit drove him into the desert (Mark 1:12), and from there he returned "filled with the power of the Spirit" and went back to Galilee (Lk 4:14). Jesus refers to himself the words of the prophet Isaiah: "The

Spirit of the Lord is upon me; he has anointed me" (61:1; Lk 4:18, 21). The scribes are guilty of blasphemy when they call his exorcisms works of one who is possessed; theirs is a sin against the Holy Spirit for which there is no pardon in all eternity, while the other offenses and blasphemies of mankind will be forgiven (Mk 3:28–30).

In John's Gospel the Holy Spirit as a person is much more clearly depicted. Especially in the discourses on the Paraclete it is often stated that after the departure of Jesus the disciples will be given another counselor. In John 14:16f we read: "I will ask the Father and he will give you another advocate who will be with you forever. He is the truth-giving Spirit." Of this Advocate we read a few verses later: "He will teach you everything and will recall to your minds all that I have said to you" (v 26). The Spirit will carry on the revelation of Jesus by giving witness of it, making it more profound and helpful for ones living in those times.

This Advocate whom Jesus will send from his Father to his disciples, "the Spirit of truth who proceeds from the Father" (15:26), has the task of opening the eyes of the world to what sin, and rightness of heart, and judgment are (16:8)—in other words, to put forward the judging that has begun with the coming of the Son of God into our world.

The equality of the Paraclete with the Father and the Son is shown in the further statement in John: "He will not speak of his own impulse: he will proclaim the message that has been given to him . . . he will derive from me what he tells you. All that the Father has is mine; that is why I have said: he takes from what is mine and gives it to you" (16:13–15). The Spirit has personal character, as the Father and the Son are persons. What is said in these discourses on the Paraclete about the work of these other helpers can hardly be understood as simple personification; they presume an actual person other than themselves. He is not only a gift, a "something"; he is a "someone" who acts.

It is also interesting to see that already in the much earlier letters of Paul the Spirit evidences details as a person, and not only in the later writing of John's Gospel. The body of the Christian is a temple of the Holy Spirit who lives in it (1 Cor 6:19); God sent the Spirit of his Son into the heart of the one who believes, the Spirit who cries Abba, Father (Gal 4:6), the Spirit comes to the aid of our weakness. The Spirit himself intercedes for us with groans beyond all utterance (Rom 8:26). Already in Paul's writings we find texts in which the Spirit is named along with the Father and the Son (1 Cor 12:4–11; 2 Cor 13:13). Later Church teaching could call on such places where the Spirit was named as the third divine person.

IX
THE HOLY CATHOLIC CHURCH,
THE COMMUNION OF SAINTS

The oldest versions of the ninth article of the profession of faith simply say: The holy Church. Toward the end of the fourth century the second adjective "catholic" was added, the meaning being that it was a universal, world-encompassing church. But soon the word took on the meaning of "orthodox, true faith," in contrast to the sects that sprang up. In the fifteenth century, in German-speaking countries catholic was equated with "Christly," a translation that is still retained in the profession of faith of the reformed church.

The origin and the meaning of the statement "communion of saints" is still disputed today. The Latin expression "sanctorum communio" can be given two meanings: "communion with all saints" or "communion with sacred things" (= sacraments). The first meaning has gotten more extensive acceptance than the second. The Church is taken to be the community of holy ones of all times, including the angels. We will look more closely whether we can find the two statements of this article in the Gospels and in what sense they are taken there.

CHURCH

The Greek word *ekklesia* found in ordinary language means an assembly of people, particularly the regular as-

103

semblies of a political community. In the New Testament
it means in most cases the name of the Christian community of the locality, or else the assembly of all Christian
faithful of the whole earth. In Paul's letters and in the Acts
of the Apostles the word nearly always means a particular
individual community. In the Gospels the word occurs only
twice, both places being in Matthew's Gospel; in 18:17 it
means a selected local community, while in 16:18 it means
the Church in general, to which all the faithful in the world
belong. In the latter case the word is in the promise that
Jesus makes to Peter after his confession that Christ is the
Messiah. "You are Peter, and on this rock I will build my
Church, and the gates of hell shall not prevail against it."

Whether Jesus actually spoke these words is disputed
today; some claim that they were attributed to Jesus later.
In the parallel text in Mark 8:27–29 these words are wanting, which shows that Matthew was responsible for their addition to the text of Mark. But Matthew was not the first to
make it up; we are dealing here with an ancient tradition-
piece that goes back to Palestinian tradition; that is, it was
originally composed in the Aramaic language. The play-
on-words, Peter–petra, makes sense only in that language,
in which the word *kephas* can mean the name of a person as
well as the word for a rock. The background of the sentence is also semitic. "The powers of the underworld" (as
the phrase is often given in translation) are given in the
original text as "the gates of Hades," which means the region of the dead and denotes really the perishability of all
things earthly.

Nevertheless it is quite doubtful whether Jesus himself
used the word "Church." The usual meaning of the expression is certainly more recent than the designation of the locality of an individual community as Paul understands the
word in his letters. Moreover the use of the future tense "I

will build my Church" presumes the resurrection of Jesus. Likewise reference to a later time is inferred in the fact that the Church is seen as an institution to last until the end of time. The earthly Jesus proclaims the reign of God which has come on earth by his very presence.

Hence it is quite likely that the word *ekklesia* was first applied to an old Palestinian Christian community, perhaps one where Peter once lived and worked. The members of the community wished to strengthen the primacy of Peter, given also by the Synoptics, by recording the promise of Jesus of building his Church on the rock Peter as a statement coming directly from the Savior himself. It is indeed possible that Jesus could have explained to his disciples the meaning of the name of Peter, which otherwise is not obvious.

Even if the word "Church" is found seldom in the Gospels, and perhaps does not go back to Jesus himself, this does not mean that the idea concerned was unknown to the evangelists. In their writings we certainly find no developed teaching about the Church as we now take the meaning of the word. But especially in John's Gospel do we find the beginning of such teaching. It is strongly indicated in the Fourth Gospel that every individual person attains salvation by faithful following of Christ. There are also many passages wherein the idea of a Church is more or less evident. For example in 11:52 we read that Jesus must gather again the scattered children of God; more clearly the Greek text says "to a leading-together." This means to a churchly community.

In the great prayer of Jesus to the Father in Chapter 17, Jesus prays not only for his disciples; he prays also for all "who are to find faith in me through their word. That they may all be one, that they may be one in us, as you, Father, are in me, so that the world may come to believe that it is you who have sent me" (17:20f). This is a prayer for the Church to come. The strong emphasis put on fraternal charity by John points to the building of a community. He never speaks of love of neighbor; his reference is always to love of the brethren, which indicates that love must be practiced before all in the community, which becomes an abode of love. The Johannine picture of the Church is a community of people in which the risen One works through his Spirit; it is the community of those to whom he gives the new life in faith and sacrament. For John the sacraments are the bequest of the unique salvific work of Jesus for all later believers in the home of the Church.

In the pastoral discourse (John 10), the idea of the Church comes out again and again. It is the duty of the good shepherd to give his life for his sheep, but he also has other sheep who do not belong to this fold; he must bring them in too: "They will listen to my voice, so there will be one fold and one shepherd" (10:15f). "This fold" means Israel; he does not say where the other sheep, who are not of this fold, come from. But it is clear enough that the Gentiles are meant. The "one fold" that will be formed when all the sheep are joined together under one shepherd is the Church, made up of Jews and Gentiles, about whose formation Luke tells us in the Acts of the Apostles.

HOLY CHURCH

Two adjectives are used to describe the Church more closely in the ninth article of the symbol: holy and catholic. The addition of the word "holy" ties this article more closely with the preceding one in which faith in the Holy Spirit is professed. Holiness constitutes the essence of the Spirit; the Church is called "holy" not because it consists only of holy members or because it gives them the means needed to attain holiness, but because it is the work of the Holy Spirit. In the Old Testament "holy" is the mark for the true being of God, his exaltation, majesty, and sublimity over all creatures. The New Testament calls Jesus holy in order to describe his divine nature. Because Jesus was begotten of the Holy Spirit and through the power of the Most High, Mary's child was called holy and the Son of God (Lk 1:35).

Through our confession of the "holy" Church we also express that it is the chosen people of God, sanctified through the death of Christ and through the Holy Spirit. There is no single text in the Gospels that describes the churchly community as one of holiness. But in his letters Paul does so often—for example, 1 Corinthians 1:2: "To those who have been sanctified in Jesus Christ, and called to be holy: with all those who invoke the name of our Lord Jesus Christ." In the post-Pauline Epistle to the Ephesians, composed about the year 90 A.D., there is particular reference to the holiness of the Church. Christ loved the Church and gave his life for it, "to make it holy . . . by washing it with water with a form of words, so that . . . it would be glorious with no speck of wrinkle or anything like that, but holy and spotless" (5:25–27).

In the prayer of Jesus for his disciples that has been quoted in the previous section, the evangelist John has the Lord praying: "Keep them holy through the truth. . . . And I dedicate myself for their sakes, that they too may be dedicated through the truth" (17:17–19). "Dedicate" or "sanctify" is here an expression used in Offertory prayers in the Old Testament, and refers to the blessing of sacrificial victims and of priests for their office. As he was himself priest and victim, so should the disciples of Jesus also be. We see that the word "sanctify" is not used in exactly the same sense as in the Creed. There is a similarity to the extent that it deals with sanctification through Jesus and the Spirit, while the discourse does not deal with ethical holiness.

The second added adjective that our article in the symbol uses here, "catholic," is not found in the New Testament. The expression "catholic Church" is found first in a letter of Ignatius of Antioch (about the year 110 A.D.), to those living in Smyrna (8:2): "Where the bishop comes, there the community should be, just as, where Christ Jesus is, there is the catholic Church." This means: where the bishop is the head of the individual community, so is Christ the head of the catholic Church. The word does not yet have the meaning of "orthodox" or "correct faith," though in its first use this is indicated since Ignatius uses it in connection with heretical groups who separated themselves from the bishop of the place.

THE COMMUNION OF SAINTS

The meaning of this second statement of the article is not yet clearly determined or definitely established. The most common interpretation sees in it simply an extension of the preceding statement: whoever belongs to the holy catholic Church is in communion with all members of the Church, those still living and those who have died. This explanation that was expressed by outstanding Christians through many centuries is certainly not wrong. Probably, though, the original meaning of the word was something else; rather than just the communion with holy people in the Church, it meant participation in holy things, in the sacraments that are made available to the members of the Church. Texts from the Gospels can be cited to illustrate both these meanings.

Understood as relating to persons, this statement is simply an explanation of the "holy Church." All people who belong to the Church make up a religious unity, even those members of the Church who have departed this earthly life, whether they are already united with Christ or may be still awaiting that meeting with him while now in purgatory. We derive this from the view of the body of Christ as being made up of members who are the individual Christians. This idea is found most of all in the letters in the New Testament (cf. 1 Cor 12:12–27; Rom 12:4f), and is older than the Gospels. Among the evangelists, we find again that it is John who tells us of the unity of Jesus with the faithful: not indeed expressly in the words of the article in the Creed, but certainly in the content of his thought. Particularly the word-picture of the true vine and its branches (Jn 15:1–8) illustrates this. Here Jesus compares himself with the vine-stalk, cared for by a vinedresser who is the heavenly Father. The disciples to whom this discourse is addressed have already been dressed by the word of Jesus; if they remain in him, he will remain in them. And only if they remain in him, like the branches on the vine, will they bear fruit.

In this discourse Jesus is not speaking as simply an earthly being looking back on his work; he is the risen One expressing his care for the post-paschal community. That community is cleansed, not in an ethical sense, but because it belongs basically to the state of salvation and because it believes the revelation that Jesus has brought. The author brings up a favorite word of the Johannine letters in his admonition: "Remain in me" (v 4). If the disciples love each other they remain in this communion with Jesus and the other members (vv 9–12). The text does not say explicitly that the union with Jesus is not broken by death, but this does follow from the whole passage.

PARTAKING OF THE SACRAMENTS

The Church is holy because it represents a community
of holy persons; the Church is also holy because it confers
the sacraments by which the people become members of
the Church and by which they can strengthen and renew
their life with Christ. Here we must speak of two sacraments: baptism and the Eucharist.

Baptism

Besides the mandate to baptize (Mt 28:19), the dialogue of Jesus with Nicodemus (Jn 3:1–12) is particularly
concerned with this theme. It does not have any inner unity
with the rest of the chapter. Verses 13–21 and 31–36 no
longer belong to the discourse; the evangelist added them
to the opening section as a kind of homily or kerygmatic
discourse. The other verses, 22–30, do not belong to this
chapter at all. One might even ask whether the verses 1–12
give us an actual dialogue of Jesus with Nicodemus, or
whether they are likewise something composed by the
evangelist. That such a conversation is possible is evident
from the matter discussed. It is about a question of salvation, and this was *the* question foremost in the minds of
those living in the time of Jesus. We see this from Mark
10:17, where a man asks Jesus: "Good Master, what must I
do to gain eternal life?" We also see it from the request of
the good thief at the crucifixion: "Jesus, remember me
when you come into your kingdom" (Lk 23:42).

Nicodemus is presented as a leader among the Jews.
The praise that he gives Jesus shows that he considered
him to be one sent by God. Before he could state the matter
that had brought him to Jesus, Jesus said to him: "Amen,
amen, I say to you: unless a man is born anew he cannot

see the kingdom of God" (Jn 3:3). This is the only place in the Fourth Gospel where we find the expression "kingdom of God" so frequently used by the Synoptics. The meaning is probably the heavenly, supreme reign into which Jesus leads those who follow him. The expression "born anew" could just as well be translated "begotten from above." The word used in the original text, *anothen,* has a double meaning: understood in a spatial sense it means from above, coming from heaven, while in a temporal sense it means from the beginning, again. Since in all other places where the evangelist uses the word it refers to position, it should be understood in this sense also in John 3:3. Hence "above" here means the heavenly, divine world by whose power mankind also must be renewed. This concept was known to the Jews, and so also Nicodemus must have understood it; being himself a scribe, well-versed in the law, he would have known that Jesus was speaking here of something brought about by God.

But he understood the expression in the temporal sense and indicated his misunderstanding by asking a rather grotesque question: "How can a man who is already old be reborn again? He cannot enter a second time into his mother's womb and so come to birth a second time." He was correct in considering a second birth in a bodily sense as absurd. Jesus does not answer the objection directly; he simply states what he meant by the phrase "come from heaven." He repeats his statement, beginning with the same solemn opening words, but now replaces the expression with the ambiguous phrase "from water and the spirit," thereby making a clear allusion to baptism. This is not bringing in a connection with some foreign body or alluding to some later insertion. The topic under discussion is the dialogue between Jesus and the Pharisee on the question of obtaining salvation. The condition for this is the birth from above, that is, from the divine sphere. The gift of salvation here is called "spirit"; elsewhere in John it is called "life." The communication of the spirit is dependent on the exaltation of Jesus; evidence of this is seen in the remark of the evangelist: "The spirit had not yet been given . . . because Jesus had not yet been raised to glory" (Jn 7:39). The begetting by the spirit is associated with the death and resurrection of Jesus. According to Jn 3:15 every believer in Christ has everlasting life. Hence the begetting from above presupposes for the faithful one an attachment to the person of Jesus. Therefore it is not a strange conclusion of belief to relate this to baptism.

In this way, of necessity, the discussion of begetting by the spirit is brought to the sacramental level. The natural result is for the believing one to gain access to Jesus in the sacrament of baptism. In that sacrament a person is given a share in Christ's saving work; in it eternal life is given.

That the interest of the evangelist was not in the external rite by which the sacrament is conferred is obvious; his concern is in the birth in the spirit. Nor do we have to assume that Jesus himself was trying to explain to Nicodemus the necessity of baptism for salvation. As in all the discourses of Jesus that we find in the Fourth Gospel, we must realize here that the language and the theology of the author had an influence in the way in which the words of Jesus are given to us.

As the discourse continues, the reader of the Gospel is told that this wonderful birth from on high is possible and also necessary. The possibility of birth in the spirit is illustrated by a comparison with the wind (the Greek word *pneuma* means "wind" as well as "spirit"). The movement of the wind is observable with the senses, but its source and its end cannot be established (at least they could not in those days before meteorological science). Likewise for those begotten of the spirit: an unbeliever cannot know how this birth comes about (that is, by the spirit of God) and to whence it goes (to eternal life).

When Nicodemus still spoke of his lack of comprehension (v 9), Jesus said to him ironically: You are a famous teacher in Israel, an authority in explaining the Scriptures, and you do not know this? This is about the same as saying: A teacher of Israel *cannot* give an explanation; he has to refuse to consider the deciding question about entry into the kingdom of God.

Eucharist

The Eucharist is the second sacrament in which the believer in Christ has a share and which attests his membership in the community of the Church. All four of the Gospels speak of this sacrament. The Synoptics tell us how Jesus gave himself as food to his disciples under the species of bread and wine at the Last Supper. These accounts are above all valuable to us because they tell us of the institution of the sacrament and tell us of the command that Jesus gave to celebrate it again and again in his memory (cf. Lk 22:19). But in what follows these discourses in the Synoptics will not be given special mention; the main interest will be on a passage in John's Gospel, which reads like a commentary on the institution narratives and gives us a real communion-instruction: John 6:42–58.

It is noteworthy that John, who gives such extensive treatment of the Last Supper of Jesus with his disciples, does not mention the institution of the Eucharist. Evidently he assumes that his readers are familiar with those details. Hence in Chapter 6 he adds to the accounts of the multiplication of the loaves a discourse on the bread of life. In this he opens up for his hearers the more profound meaning of the multiplication of the bread, and at the end he tells of the effect of the discourse on the people.

The Multiplication of the Loaves
(John 6:1–15)

The evangelists tell us six times of the feeding of a crowd of people by Jesus. Mark and Matthew each tell twice of such a miracle. Luke and John each give only one such report. The more common opinion today is that Jesus performed such a miracle for those who came to hear his words only once, but that the account of this meal was soon in circulation in traditional writings in two versions. John's account has great similarity with the first report of Mark (6:35–44), but still departs from it on many points. This gives reason to assume that the fourth evangelist knew of an account that sounded much like the one Mark knew, and that John then wrote his own version from this second source.

All the New Testament accounts of this meal are written along the lines of similar narratives in the Old Testament—the feeding of the people of Israel in the desert by Moses (Ex 16) and the miracle of the bread of the prophet Elisha, who fed one hundred men with twenty loaves (2 Kgs 4:42–44). Jesus' miracle is certainly more remarkable than those of his prophetic predecessors. Moses had to pray to God that he might feed his people. And in contrast to the one hundred people that Elisha fed, Jesus fed five thousand, and with only five loaves, rather than the twenty that the Old Testament prophet had. Moreover, there were twelve baskets left over in the miracle of Jesus.

John tells of the miracle indirectly: he says that Jesus divided the five loaves and two fish among the five thousand, and all could eat of them as much as they wanted. In saying before the sharing of the bread that Jesus gave thanks (*eucharistesas*), this is perhaps a reference to the eucharistic bread of the sacrament. In asking them to collect the fragments after the meal so that nothing should be spoiled, he is indicating a higher food that never spoils "but remains for eternal life" (v 27).

John's discourse is neither an historically accurate report nor a freely-invented story. An historical kernel can be seen; the evangelist stresses the miraculous character of the meal. But the main point is the reference to more profound truths: Jesus is the eternal ambassador of God, the Messiah, the great one, the prophet far superior to Moses; he is indeed the bread come down from heaven, as the discourse of the bread discloses in what follows.

However, he first brings in the account of the walking on water (6:16–21), as Mark 6:45–51 tells also of such a miracle after the miracle of the bread. According to Mark, Jesus comes to help, walking across the water to the disciples when they were in danger of drowning; in John's account the saving help is given in order to reveal his divine nature. In Mark he discloses that he is the Master of the disciples with the words: "Take courage. It is I! Do not be afraid!" (6:50). In almost the same words in John 6:20 it is a revelation of his own divinity. In putting the story of the walking on water in his sixth chapter the evangelist's purpose is to show that this miracle has meaning also for the Eucharist. In the multiplication of the loaves Jesus shows that he has power over the bread; by walking on the water he is saying that with his body he can break the laws of the corporeal world. Both are necessary for the Eucharist.

The Eucharistic Discourse
(6:22–59)

Very early in the Church the multiplication of the loaves was understood as a reference to the Eucharist. It was told with variations that were needed to accord with the actions of Jesus at the Last Supper (cf. Mk 8:6; 14:22). Only John, however, gives us a long discourse about the meaning of the event, and in his discourse we hear Jesus speaking at length on the meaning of the sacramental meal, in language altogether in the style of the evangelist. Somewhat astonishing also is the chorus-response of the people forming part of the discourse and so influencing the train of thought.

All this goes to show that here John is not giving us a record of an actual speech of Jesus; here the evangelist is the prime author. With such a speech Jesus would have demanded too much of his audience; they would simply not have been able to understand what he was saying. Only faithful Christians in post-resurrection times would have been able to understand what was going on. The discourse is not directed at Galilean fellow citizens of Jesus; the intended audience were the doubting Christians who claimed to be in union with God and Christ without partaking of the Eucharist. This is why the discourse puts such insistent stress on the need of receiving the body and blood of the Lord.

Whether the last section (vv 51c–58) comes from the author himself or whether it was added later by those who published his work is still disputed by exegetes. The claims for originality of these verses seem to have the better grounds. One of the strongest of these claims is that verse 31 cites a verse of a psalm (Ps 78:24): "He gave them bread from heaven to eat." Verses 32–47 then explain "bread from heaven," and verses 48–58 go on to explain "he gave them to eat." The trains of thought run parallel in the two sections.

The content also shows the original unity of the discourse. The first part tells us where Jesus is; then the second part explains what he gives to those who follow him. In other words: the first part deals with the faith through which we find Jesus, and the second part tells us of the Eucharist, the means whereby we share with him.

The first part (vv 26–47) begins with the admonition not to be overly concerned about earthly food; they should show care for the food that continually affords eternal life. Hence there is a demand for faith in the One sent by God. But the Jews wanted to give this faith only if Jesus would work a confirming miracle for them. They considered the multiplication of the loaves as insufficient. Jesus should have bread rain down from heaven as once Moses did for the people in the desert. Jesus counters this objection by saying that it was his heavenly Father, not Moses, who gave the bread from heaven; he himself is the living bread come down from heaven. Then Jesus explains what faith is: to acknowledge him as the One sent by the Father.

To this his listeners objected: How can Jesus be the One who has come from heaven when we know where he lives and who his parents are? To this Jesus answers: Faith is a special gift of God; only those can come to Jesus whom the Father draws to himself; only the one who listens to Jesus can come to know the Father.

In the second part of the discourse (vv 48–58) the effect of bread from heaven is spoken of: it brings us "eternal life." The Israelites who ate manna in the desert died there, but the one who eats the bread of life, which is Jesus himself, will have eternal life. Eating the bread of life means eating the body of Jesus. Naturally his hearers repudiated this idea, but Jesus did not take it back. He repeated it in stronger terms: only those who eat the flesh of Jesus and drink his blood will have life. This food brings about the presence of Jesus in them and their union with him; by it they gain a living bond with him. Verse 58 which closes this second part of the discourse again takes up the thought of verse 50: the person who eats this bread which came down from heaven will not die like those of our forefathers who died in the wilderness; he will live eternally.

Taking the whole discourse as a unit, it gives us a word-picture and a promise of the Eucharist. Seen one way, Jesus is the bread of life because he brings all of revelation; but he is also the One who brings us life in the sacramental gift of the Eucharist. In him we share the salvation event that comes to believers as a result of his incarnation and his death on the cross. The faithful communicant of the Eucharist-gift, which is the risen Christ, also becomes one who receives a share in the saving work of Jesus and the everlasting life which is the fruit of his sacrifice.

From this we see that verses 51 through 58 of John 6 are actually an instruction on the salvation-necessity and the grace-bestowal of the Eucharist, an instructive text that goes far beyond all other eucharistic texts of the New Testament. The "mystery of faith" that John tries to bring home to us in this pericope encapsulates also a profound sense of the communion of saints; this mystery gives us union with Christ and with all members of the Church.

Eucharistic interpretation of John 6:51–58 was and is now disputed among exegetes. Even among Catholic teachers, followers of Augustine and Origin, there was a strong group who interpreted the "eating of the body of Christ" in an exaggerated sense. For them it meant "to attach oneself through faith to the sacrifice of Christ."

Adherents of a spiritual, non-eucharistic interpretation of the text are inclined to base their opinions on John 6:63, where the author has Jesus tell us: "Only the spirit gives life; the flesh is of no avail. The words I have been speaking to you are spirit and life." Here, though, "spirit" does not mean a spiritual, overdrawn understanding of the Scripture; the reference is to the divine spirit, designated already in the Old Testament as a life-giving one. And "flesh" here does not exclude a literal meaning; it says: human weakness, or natural human understanding, can never arrive at an understanding of Jesus in the Eucharist.

Another interpretation of the text applies flesh and spirit to the two different modes of existence of Jesus: in his earthly mode of presence he cannot fulfill his promise to give us his body to eat; he can do this only in his heavenly existence. "The words I have been speaking to you" (v 63b) do not refer only to the concluding verse; they refer to the whole eucharistic discourse. For the faithful person all that Jesus has said in the discourse means spirit and life. One cannot distort this statement by limiting it as applying only to a eucharistic understanding of the preceding verse.

X
FORGIVENESS OF SINS

The tenth article of the apostolic symbol professes that believers can receive forgiveness of their sins in the Church. In the eastern Church this article is often expressed as: I believe in a baptism for forgiveness of sins. In the western Church the question remains open whether it means remission of sin that is joined with baptism, or whether sins committed after baptism are also remitted.

Remission of sins is spoken of in many places in the Gospels. According to Mark 1:4 John the Baptist preached "a baptism of conversion for the remission of sins." Whether the conversion (often translated less correctly as "penance") is the source of the forgiveness of sins or whether the baptism of penance effects the conversion cannot be stated with certainty. In his healing miracles Jesus often declared the forgiveness of sins of the sick person along with the cure of the sickness.

Jesus conferred the power "to bind and to loose" on Peter according to Matthew 16:19, and with that power also assurance that his word would have value in heaven. This "transfer of the power of the keys" does not mean explicitly the power to forgive sins. It means the ability to decide what the right teaching is and what is wrong, and also to explain who can become a participant by reception in the Church of salvation.

Matthew 18:18 is a parallel to 16:19; here all disciples are assured that "all that you bind on earth shall be bound in heaven, and all that you loose on earth shall be loosed in heaven." According to this text the Church and every local community has the power to decide who belongs to it and who does not. Divine authority stands behind its decision because its word has value in heaven. But because the Church not only has power to bind, and because the power to loose has also been given to it, the exclusion of a sinner from it must not be final; the possibility of being received again is left open. Without question the power to forgive sins is contained in the statement of Matthew 18:18.

However, from the directly preceding text (vv 15–17) all members of the Church have a responsibility to one another. If a member sins, another member should first go and advise the sinner of the fault committed, suggesting corrections to be applied. If the sinner will not listen to the first friend, then two or three others should be brought in as witnesses to help bring about the correction. If that proves useless, then the fault should be spoken of in the community. But if the sinner will not listen to the community either, then the member can no longer be considered as belonging to the community, but must be regarded as a pagan or a tax collector. This "order of the community" that Matthew speaks of has all the faithful, and not only the superior, having an interest that the sinner should gain pardon for his sin or be denied that pardon. That the fraternal correction here recommended is no longer practiced is regrettable; such correction now is regarded as altogether the task of the official Church. Sacramental penance and the corresponding extra-sacramental admonitions should work together to make it possible for a Christian who has sinned to regain admission to a living community in the Church.

The two texts from Matthew that have been discussed thus far speak rather in general of the power to forgive sins. In John's Gospel we find a text that deals explicitly with the subject. It is the account of the appearance of the risen Savior to his disciples in the evening of Easter Day (20:19–23).

They are assembled behind closed doors out of fear of the Jews. But the risen Jesus has the power to show himself to them in his glorified body. "He came and stood there in their midst. 'Peace be to you,' he said." He came of his own accord; they did not expect him. The peace that he wished them is the true Easter gift of Jesus. It does not mean a kind of interior feeling, the kind that a person can feel when conscious of no serious offense of the soul against God. Here "peace" means reconciliation of all the world that his death on the cross has effected between God and mankind.

Then he showed them his hands and his side. This showing of the wounded places that Jesus wished to keep on his glorified body should convince his disciples that the risen One is the same as the crucified One. The One standing in their midst was not a bodiless shade; he is the One whose body was tortured on the cross and lay in the tomb, now returned with new life. He is no longer subject to the laws of space and time; he has been raised to the majesty and glory of his divine nature.

"Thus the disciples saw the Lord and were glad." This Easter peace wipes out doubt and fear and terror. Evidently Jesus was able to convince his disciples of the reality of his resurrection. He repeated his greeting wish, and added: "As the Father sent me, so I am sending you." The one sent represents the sender: he is entirely in his service and possesses his omnipotence. This mission that begins with Jesus as the one sent by the Father is passed on to the disciples: they are representatives of Jesus and share in his power.

With that he breathed on them and said: "Receive the

Holy Spirit!" Being empowered with the Holy Spirit is joined with their mission. This action of Jesus reminds us of Genesis 2:7: God the Creator made man from the dust of the earth and blew the breath of life into his nostrils, and so the man became a living being. In Genesis the meaning is simply natural life. On Easter Day the bestowal of the Spirit refers to the "new life," the "new person." Already in Ezekiel's prophecy we read: "I shall give you a new heart and put a new spirit in you. . . . I shall put my spirit in you and make you keep my laws and observe carefully my commandments" (36:26f). The same prophet joins cleansing from offenses with the in-pouring of the holy spirit (36:25).

After telling of Jesus' breathing on the disciples, John gives us the important words of the risen Savior: "When you forgive men's sins, they are forgiven; when you hold them bound, they are held bound." In the original text the discourse is of sins "released" and "retained." These are expressions corresponding to the "bind" and "loose" of Matthew 18:18. There, as we have seen, the authority given the meaning is mediation of salvation in general. In John the words must be understood in a narrower sense: they refer to forgiveness of sins (and refusing that forgiveness). As a kind of other Easter gift the Savior empowers his disciples and gives them the mandate to reconcile the faithful to God through forgiveness of sins.

It can be questioned whether here John is speaking of the sacrament of reconciliation, as he speaks (3:5) of baptism and (6:51ff) of the Eucharist. Theologians are divided in their opinions on this. If one should wish to draw no more from the text than it offers directly, we would have to say that the evangelist speaks here of a special power that was handed over to the Church: to confer forgiveness of sins, or to deny that forgiveness. It does not disclose where or how this power will be used. The basic efficacy of the

Church "to administer the sacrament of reconciliation" is asserted, but no explicit advice is given about actual use of that power. There is also dispute about the question whether the community as a whole is the one holding this power, or whether it belongs only to the superior.

The First Epistle of John, which was composed at about the same time as the Fourth Gospel and comes certainly from the same milieu, speaks of a confession of sin and a corresponding forgiveness (1:9). The same epistle (5:16) exhorts the community to pray for the erring brother, "and God will give life to all whose sin does not lead to death." The author excludes mortal sin in his appeal for intercession. He probably means extremely serious sins, something like total loss of faith, but he does not say they are unforgivable. From this we can conclude that in the community of John there was a forgiveness and a reservation of absolution of sin, which probably derives from John 20:22. The community could not be capricious about absolving or not absolving from sin. Only when a sinner will not fulfill the necessary conditions for forgiveness, conversion and contrition must the absolution be denied. A confession before the community or its leader was required before a rightful judgment could be made.

In the course of the centuries the practice of reconciliation has undergone considerable development. There have been and there still are different forms in use. The basic teaching for them all is the mandate given by the risen One in John 20:22f.

XI
RESURRECTION OF THE DEAD

This article of the formal profession of faith was in earlier times put in the words: I believe in the resurrection of the flesh. The earlier form expresses somewhat more meaningfully than the modern ecumenical version that we are not dealing with some kind of transferred sense of resurrection; there is to be a real resurrection of the whole person, body and soul, but of course not a return to the earthly life that we have come to know. However, it is not simply continued existence of the soul. We profess rather that the body is also an essential part of our human being and should have a part in our incorruptibility and exaltation.

Hence the article of the Creed was originally directed against the teaching of the Greek philosophers who did not consider the body to be essential to the person; they saw it as a kind of prison of the soul, from which the soul had to be freed in order to attain its proper being.

Faith in the resurrection of the body is found only in the latest books of the Old Testament—for example, Daniel 12:2: "Of those who sleep in the dust of the earth many will awake, some of them to eternal life, the others to shame and eternal banishment." Faith in the resurrection of the dead was professed by the Jews generally in the time of Jesus; only the Sadducees denied it. But even in early Christianity there were people who found difficulty with this faith. Paul already had to defend himself against these doubters in his First Epistle to the Corinthians.

The Synoptics (Mk 12:18–26 and parallels) tell us of a discussion that Jesus had with the Sadducees about the question of the resurrection. Their denial was not due to the influence of the Greek philosophers: they professed adherence to the words of the earlier writings of the Bible where there is nothing about such a continuation of life. Their question to Jesus was intended to bring ridicule, as was customary among the scribes when they wanted to call attention to a difficulty. The one they brought up in this case was the in-law marriage situation described in Deuteronomy 25:5ff. If an Israelite dies without male offspring, his brother must marry the widowed sister-in-law. The first son of this marriage should then carry on the name of the brother who had died. In ancient times this law had some meaning for carrying on posterity, but it had lost its force long before the Savior's time. The question of the Sadducees was altogether hypothetical, but to them it seemed a suitable one to assail the faith in the resurrection. One expected to enjoy heightened earthly joys in the world to come, and hence also to have the joys of marriage and family life. Assuming that the in-law marriage would have to be repeated several times because none of the seven brothers received a son to continue the line of the first-born one, the question was: Which one's wife would the woman be in the life beyond?

Jesus gave a serious answer to the mockery of the questioners. Actually they did not understand the Scripture; most of all, they did not see that God is more powerful than human understanding can imagine. The laws of this world no longer hold after the resurrection from the dead. There will not be any marital relations between husband and wife, no more marrying and giving in marriage. The bodiliness of those who have risen will not be the same as that of those living on earth. There they will be "like the angels in heaven." In later times this comparison with the angels in heaven led to a cheapening of sexuality and marriage by Christian theologians.

But this would be a misunderstanding of Jesus' words: their intent is to show that the body is also saved in the resurrection and that the whole person, with all its natural faculties, is raised to an other-worldly existence. This does indeed exclude sexual participation, but not the love between those who were marriage partners on earth.

In opposition to the Sadducees Jesus maintains that there is actual resurrection of the dead. For this he cites scriptural proof. At the apparition in the burning bush (Ex 3:1ff), Yahweh appeared to Moses as the God of Abraham, Isaac, and Jacob. But he is not a god of the dead, he is God of the living. This does not seem to be a very convincing demonstration. But the text does indeed indicate that this manifestation of Yahweh points to the fact that the patriarchs are still alive. One can say more correctly that in this reference to the ancients of the Jews Jesus wanted to remind them of God's faithfulness in carrying out the promise that he had given them that they would have a rich posterity and an enduring inheritance (Gen 15:1ff). Bodiliness belongs to complete happiness for an Israelite. Hence the promise of God cannot be fulfilled by a life that ends with death. The answer of Jesus is not exegetical hairsplitting; it is a consequence of God's faithfulness to his covenant.

Another statement of Jesus that gives witness to his belief in the resurrection of the dead is found only in Luke's Gospel (14:14). At a meal to which Jesus had been invited he said to his host that when he gave a dinner or supper, he should not invite friends or relatives or neighbors who were rich and who would invite him in return. Rather, he should give hospitality to those who could not make him any return. Then "he would have his reward when the just return again"—that is, God himself would reward him. We cannot conclude from this statement that Jesus did not know of a general resurrection and that he only knew of resurrection for souls of the just, as was the late-Jewish belief. He does indeed proceed from the supposition that only for those who are good will there be a happy ending. Luke 13:27f shows that he reckoned with eternal punishment for evildoers: the patriarchs and prophets would sit at table with the Gentiles in the kingdom of God while the unbelieving contemporaries of Jesus would be left outside.

The belief in the general resurrection of all the dead finds expression often in John's Gospel, most of all in Chapter 5, where there are texts that speak clearly of it. But in the same context there are other passages where the future resurrection at the end of the world is confused with the present. Many interpreters see such a contradiction between these texts that they believe them to come from a different author. These interpreters say that the evangelist of the Fourth Gospel knew only of a resurrection in present time; the places where there is talk of a future resurrection have been added by a later hand in order to prevent a misunderstanding of the teaching of the author.

The adoption of additions to the original text of the Gospel is not at all unthinkable. Today it is generally accepted that Chapter 21 was added only after the death of the author. Hence it is quite possible that shorter passages by a later hand also have found their way into the text. It is a different question whether the evangelist basically denies the teaching of a resurrection at the end of time or whether this can be brought into agreement with his theology. Let us look more closely at the texts.

In John 5:25 we read: "Believe me when I tell you this, the time is coming, *and it is already here,* when the dead will listen to the voice of God, and those who listen to it will live." This means that the decision on the destiny of the person in the time hereafter has already begun: it has already come about in the person and the revelation of Jesus. Belief or disbelief in Jesus decides already while we are on earth what will be the coming destiny of the human person. There is resurrection already in this present time when the person accepts the Gospel in faith and thus awakens from the spiritual death-sleep. This is the meaning of the words: "Whoever listens to my words and puts his trust in him who has sent me enjoys eternal life. He does not meet with rejection; he has passed already from death to life" (5:24).

But only a few lines later we read: "The time is coming when all those who are in their graves will hear his voice and *will* come out of them: those whose actions have been good will rise to new life and those whose doings have been evil will rise to meet their sentence" (5:28f). This does not explicitly mention resurrection of the body, but it presumes this where it says that "those who are in their graves" will come out of them.

The view would hardly be wrong to say that these and similar texts that relate to a coming resurrection are not words of the original evangelist. They are very probably attributable to the Johannine school which published the Gospel of their master. They have surely not understood their master so poorly as to believe that he wished to displace the traditional teaching about the future resurrection by his concept of the one in present time. The "eternal life" that the faithful believer already has attains its final completion in the resurrection from the dead. The same holds for unbelievers: it means death already here on earth and a resurrection "to judgment." We are not given a description of the resurrection from the dead, but it is presumed.

Hence we can say that the Gospel passage of 5:28f does

not imply a correction of the actual eschatology of the evangelist; it aims only to amplify it. The Johannine school wishes to pronounce against the heretical views that allow the resurrection from the dead to have reference only to the present, without any reference to a future one, and they wished to guard the assertions of their master against misuse. Paul also had to express opposition to such views among the Christians of Corinth (1 Cor 15:12f); the later letter, 2 Timothy, warns against the "meaningless talk" of certain people who maintained that the resurrection had already occurred (2:16–18).

XII
AND ETERNAL LIFE

The last article of the apostolic symbol professes the faith in eternal life. In the great Creed of Constantinople the two last articles are combined; there we read: We await the resurrection of the dead and the life in the world to come. In this way we say that through the final resurrection of the dead the present age of the world comes to an end and in its place something completely new enters: an existence that is eternal, one that takes away the limits of time and space. As there is a resurrection to life and one to judgment (Jn 5:29), so also the life after death is not the same for everyone. For those whose actions have been good this means eternal happiness, and for the others, eternal punishment. In the symbol this is not expressly stated, but it is presupposed as distinct teaching of the New Testament.

"Eternal life" as a description of future happiness in the world to come is found already in the Synoptic Gospels, though rather rarely. Jesus promises this reward to all those who leave everything for his sake to follow him; they will receive reward a hundredfold: "Now in this world a hundred times their worth, houses, sisters, brothers, mothers, children, and lands, but with persecution; and in the world to come they will receive everlasting life" (Mk 10:29f).

In a discourse on the judgment of the world, Matthew gives a clear statement of the different destinies of people in life to come (25:31–46). To those standing at his right hand, the ones who have practiced love of neighbor and have been placed at his right hand, the Son of Man awards the kingdom that was prepared for them since the beginning of the world. To those standing at his left he assigns everlasting fire as their place of residence. The final statement reads: "And these (the unmerciful ones) shall pass on to eternal punishment, but the virtuous to eternal life" (v 46). This eternal life is clearly an expression for the final happiness that God gives his faithful servants (cf. Mt 25:21–23). Its duration is forever, as also is the punishment for those who have not been merciful.

The expression "eternal life" is particularly frequent in John's Gospel. But it is not used exclusively for happiness in the world to come; often it expresses the state of grace of the faithful on this earth. In the account of the raising of Lazarus there is a dialogue of Jesus with Martha, the sister of the man who had died. It tells clearly how what is eschatological, what deals with life after death, has a continuing relation to the present. When Jesus came to Bethany, Lazarus had already been four days in the grave. Martha said to Jesus: "Lord, if you had been here, my brother would not have died." Jesus answered: "Your brother will rise again," to which Martha replied: "I know that he will rise again at the resurrection when the last day comes." Jesus answered her: "I am the resurrection and the life" (Jn 11:21–25). With this sublime "I-am" statement Jesus gives witness that he is the One to whom God has given the power of giving life. Resurrection has come already through the presence of Jesus. Whoever listens faithfully to his voice that has now sounded has completed the step into the province of God's life and will die no more in eternity. The eternal life is already present in the believer and lives on without a break at bodily death.

In the farewell discourse in John (Chapters 14

through 17), the Old Testament expression "that day" is
given a new content by the evangelist. Originally it meant
the day of Yahweh, that is, the end of days, the great judgment day. John understands it to be the time after the resurrection of Jesus; it is the time when, after he has been
taken up to God, he appears to the disciples (cf. 14:20;
16:23, 26). Where Jesus says: "I will not leave you orphans;
I will come again to you" (14:18), there is in the background of his statement the thought of the parousia of the
Lord on the last day. However, this is not his intention
here; he is speaking of the time after the resurrection of
Jesus during which his disciples gain a deeper inner communion with him and in which he reveals himself to them
(cf. vv 21f).

This is a revision of the early Christian expectation of
the parousia. It could also mean that sometimes Jesus
comes at the death of a disciple in order to bring him to the
house of his Father. Only then will the promise to all who
believe in him be fulfilled. For the evangelist Easter is the
dawn of the eschatological "day of the Lord"; it marks the
beginning of the complete community of God. This combination of the ancient Christian expectation of the parousia with the Easter experience of the disciples is the
special theological burden of the evangelist.

It would be wrong for us to infer from what has been
said about the assertions of John's Gospel that he is denying
or correcting the teaching of the other evangelists who
speak of a final judgment, a raising from the dead, and
only after that an entry into eternal life. Only this is correctly put: for John the future things do not play a prom-
inent role. The reason for this is that he proceeds from the
historical revelation in Christ and its meaning for salvation.
Salvation or judgment is accomplished in the current decision for or against Christ. What is to come is not rejected;

it is actualized. Here and now the decision is made for the future.

This partiality in eschatology has something grand about it, but it was not maintained even by the disciples of the evangelist. They turned their attention again to the future and saw it as a necessary completion for Johannine thought.

When we Christians of today confess our faith in eternal life, we must understand it in the twofold sense which it has in the Gospels. We believe in the future life of final salvation in God. And we also believe that our future is decided here and now. Through belief in Jesus and his message we already possess the essentials of eternal life. The passage to complete happiness through death and judgment then loses its terror. Death cannot endanger the eternal life that we already possess.